# YOUR BEST YEAR

## 2·0·1·7

### PRODUCTIVITY WORKBOOK &
### ONLINE BUSINESS PLANNER

*by Lisa Jacobs*

# TABLE OF CONTENTS

# HOW TO USE THIS WORKBOOK

This is the fourth annual edition of the *Your Best Year* series, and it continues to evolve year after year. Last year's *Your Best Year 2016* was such a giant success, I thought I might simply change the dates and reproduce it.

I wondered, *how much better can it get?* With 10,000+ raving fans behind it, I could have absolutely left it "as is" and that would have been well enough.

However, I learned even more about goal-setting and business strategy as the year progressed. I tripled my email list and quadrupled my income. I shattered limitations that had been keeping me stuck for *years*.

I found more success than ever before, and because my favorite thing in business is to figure something out and then teach it to others, I knew this book was destined to evolve just as my career had.

Therefore, the *reason* for not changing anything about the book became the **challenge**:

## HOW MUCH BETTER CAN IT GET?

*So, what changed?* The short answer is this: **I did.** I changed. My results were created through a culmination of well-showcased experience, the right projects coming to a head, having the correct systems in place, and buying the necessary business training.

**There are lies we tell ourselves in business ...**

* I need to have everything perfect before I start
* I need more experience/research before it will take off
* I need to sacrifice too much time to make it work
* My brand's not perfect yet, so the rest is all for naught
* I just need a little more proof it will actually work before I go all in
* As soon as I get to [X] sales or [X] subscribers, I'll take the next step!

If any of those points ring true, I feel you. Trust me, you are not alone. I still find fear blocking my business' growth in the form of reasons, justifications, or logic.

But the reality is, these are just lies you use to keep yourself feeling safe and comfortable when what this business really wants from you is an open-minded willingness to reach your potential of unlimited expansion.

*It's always a mistake to think you can limit yourself and expand at the same time.*

In 2016, I made the decision to change. This part is so simple, that it's both scary and heartbreaking because we limit ourselves every day. I moved toward change. I made decisions as though I were already running a six-figure business … because I had to think like that successful business owner before I could become her.

I did four specific things to exceed my goals and shatter my income ceilings this year. I made …

* My goals resolute
* My strategies specific
* My system efficient
* My action plan productive

In this book, I'm going to show you how to create the same. This year's *Your Best Year* is a refresher on the fundamentals: you'll review what is and what's not working, identify what needs to change, challenge your limitations, and figure out what to focus on. Then, we're going to ask the question that shaped this book because it's the same question that shaped my entire year …

## HOW MUCH BETTER CAN IT GET?

Inside this workbook, you'll find prompts for thought-provoking, spiritual contemplation. As a community (use #yby2017 on social), we celebrate the ugly cries sponsored by the tough questions within! You'll learn how to honor and encourage your entrepreneurial ambition to reach levels you've never imagined.

You'll lay everything about your life and business on the table, take a discerning look at what's there, and decide what to keep. It's a cleansing ritual, a spring-cleaning for the soul. These exercises will create space for the action, connection, and abundance you've been craving all along.

**"** LET YOURSELF BE SILENTLY DRAWN BY THE STRONG PULL OF WHAT YOU REALLY LOVE. IT WILL NOT LEAD YOU ASTRAY. *– Rumi*

My goal for this book is to help you create the silence, identify what truly pulls you, and show you how to let that love lead. I want you to become a high-performing person who refuses to allow life to pass you by.

## BEFORE YOU GET STARTED

Here are some things you might like to gather and arrange before starting the planning exercises within this workbook.

 **#1 At least one day planner**

I run a multi-faceted creative business and two day planners help me separate the plans and goals I create. I keep a day planner for my blog (it serves as an editorial calendar and note-keeper) and another one that oversees my entire operation and schedule. I'll explain this in more detail later in the series, but in the last section, I'm going to issue important tasks for you to plug into your day planner in order to keep you on track.

 **#2 A giant drawing pad**

While you're in the paper section picking out your day planner, pick up a children's giant drawing pad also. They're typically 16"×22", and they are great for mapping out big projects and goals. You can find them in the Crayola aisle.

 **#3 Alone time**

I choose to do my annual review and intention-setting when I can find some solitude, over a period of about four days. I typically spend one to two hours in reflection, and I set the mood so that it is gentle, calm, and sober. If that's not possible for you, carve out a block of quiet time in one day.

I'll take no excuses here: make this alone time happen. I'm a married mother of four, and I'm determined to honor this sacred practice. I'll go to my bedroom and send the "do not disturb" message before I begin. Self-reflection is critical to your wellbeing. Once you start a session, you are not to be interrupted.

### #4 Space to spread out

I prefer the living room floor, but any wide-open space will do. It's always better to do planning and review exercises outside of your normal work space; it allows for fresh perspective and new ideas.

### #5 Comfort items

Be sure to have ready a delicious ice water and/or hot drink, favorite pens, and any additional resources you plan on using. If possible, turn off electronic distractions.

### #6 Pen and paper

Be sure to write down everything that occurs to you. If you stop to think about something as you reflect, record it.

When you follow the rumination of the mind without pen and paper, you chase thoughts that are too scattered to truly connect. Writing down any new ideas, problems, uncomfortable feelings, etc., lets them escape to the page where they can be reworked and shaped into successful projects or changes.

## It's time to hurdle your obstacles

How do you get from where you are to where you want to be? You physically move toward it; you take the actions necessary to get you there. If you wanted to travel from Pittsburgh to New York, you can't sit down on a park bench in Pittsburgh and wonder why you're not getting to New York.

It seems too simple to be true, but few people actively take action toward their goals. Most people are sitting on a park bench in Pittsburgh complaining about how their dreams aren't showing up for them. Can New York show up in Pittsburgh? No!

> " IF YOU DON'T LIKE WHERE YOU ARE, MOVE. YOU ARE NOT A TREE.  *– unknown*

This book is a monster, hungry for your obstacles and starved for your achievement. Are you ready to feed it?

# YOUR BEST YEAR IS HERE

This workbook contains dozens of exercises divided into three result-oriented sections.

**In section one,** you're going to explore the past year to appreciate how far you've come *and* face the obstacles that have been blocking your path. You'll then question your current limitations and set up game-changing objectives for the year ahead.

*process*

**In section two,** you'll enjoy a mix of instruction and application designed to prepare you for the exciting year ahead. You'll learn what to focus on in order to propel your business to the next level, how to trust it to provide, and how to build an annual strategy for success.

*prepare*

**In section three,** you'll find a complete system designed to help you accomplish whatever goals you set for the year.

*practice*

YOUR BEST YEAR 2017 *by Lisa Jacobs*

# INTRODUCTION

Welcome to *Your Best Year 2017: Productivity Workbook and Online Business Planner*. This is the fourth edition and my favorite thing to create every year. I love self-discovery, effective strategy, and growth-oriented results, and because I love it so, I'm honored to be part of your journey.

This is going to be an enjoyable process, but first we have to cover the difficult aspects of online business: the never-ending uncertainty and lack of validation.

## *A creative career is demanding*

Yes, I'm typing to you in my pajamas, under a blanket on my couch with a steamy cup of vanilla chai beside me. The irony is not lost on me, but I'll say it again: A creative career is demanding.

I'm Lisa Jacobs, a marketing strategist and blogger. I, too have an online business, and I make it all up as I go! I never know for sure what will sell or what will fail. I don't know if I'll get paid for the forty hours of work I've already invested into my next project. It could be all for naught; it's a wild gamble! I'll bet you can relate.

That's why *Your Best Year* was designed specifically for online entrepreneurs. It's here to be your navigational guide, personal motivator, and the keeper of your vision.

You see, it dawned on me a while back that the majority of online entrepreneurs are running their businesses day-by-day, and if you reflect on that for a moment, you'll realize how disturbing it is. This is the only industry in which small business owners try to operate, let alone succeed in such a chaotic way.

I call this frenzied approach to business "the daily scramble." Most online entrepreneurs wake up *today* and ask: "What am I going to do *today* to get more sales already?" And the scramble begins …

> "Why, I'll send an email! I'll promote this post on Facebook! I'll make four new items and list them in my storefront, and then I'll tweet and Instagram each of them so everyone will come check them out."

Sound familiar? I can promise you: a serious businessperson doesn't scramble, she schedules. A real businesswoman doesn't try something one day, check stats, and give up! No, she persists. She continues to pursue her goals.

A thriving entrepreneurship is based on seasons, and it's time to appreciate and utilize its natural rhythm. For example, one of my clients came out of a phenomenal holiday season; her sales were off-the-chart from both show and online. About two weeks later, she wrote me an email to tell me that now everything she's doing is "resulting in crickets." She's clearing flying by the seat of her pants; riding high during busy season and crash-landing as soon as it ends.

*Can you relate?*

Let's look at it another way: Her business is doing fine, but she's failing to utilize its seasons. Are you with me? This isn't about what happened last month or what online campaign didn't produce the results that you anticipated yesterday.

It is about understanding the peaks and crests of your business so that you can plan and persist accordingly. This book is designed to help you do just that.

Online business is truly the land of unlimited profit potential … *if* you're willing to do the work. You can't look at the face of an online entrepreneur's successful business and forget all that goes into the operation behind the scenes. I liken it to the workings of a car; the beautiful body you see sitting on the wheels is not what makes the machine run.

I decided that this year I was going to fine-tune that machine because I realized there was a good reason I wasn't hitting my goals.

Every December from 2010-2015, while in review and reflection, I wrote "six-figures" as a goal I'd like to accomplish. Then, I'd start to strategize the products and services I could offer to achieve that financial goal (based on the previous year's earnings), and the numbers were always askew. What I *believed* I could earn never added up to what I *wanted* to earn.

Come January, I'd slash my income goal. I told myself, "Okay. Maybe $100,000 isn't realistic at my current level. It is almost tripling the most I've ever made in a single year to date, after all. Maybe I should lower that just a tad."

I felt anxious and doubted my ability to earn such a huge and glorious figure. I concluded, "I'd be more than happy with $70,000. That's still quite a lucrative amount!"

By June, regardless of how I'd done so far that year, the slow months hit. And we all know, slow months are dismal. There was so much goal to go, but the funds trickled in. So, I negotiated my salary again. I thought, "You're nowhere near your (already compromised) goal of $70,000."

In 2015, I'd already earned my previous year's salary by July — I was close to my huge income goal — and I STILL negotiated (with myself) to allow for a lower salary because of a slow period!

I strategized, "Okay. Just be sure you double last year's salary." And guess what I did in 2015? I doubled my last year's salary. Nothing more, nothing less. Can you relate?

In 2016, I actively changed everything in my life and business that felt out of sync. Change is upending, no question, but I was tired of keeping my problems. Therefore, I didn't take it one step at a time; I jumped the entire flight of stairs.

**I looked at what I'd been struggling with for way too long.** I decided to move the needle. I schedule exercises of change into my calendar now, whether it be a workout (to lose weight and feel better in my skin) or a 90-minute power session to work on a project that will become a long-standing asset to my business.

In the last twelve months, I've completely redecorated my home to create a space that inspires me, firmly closed the door to toxic relationships in my life, stopped pinning about travel and started planning it — this year, my family visited San Francisco, New York, the Bahamas, and Disney World Orlando, PLUS I took on a creative retreat just for me! I invested thousands of dollars into my own training, taught a full-on workshop for CreativeLive, hired my first assistant, hired a bi-weekly housecleaning crew, hired a personal trainer, and hired a second assistant. I also started eating more plants!

Then, I put my beautiful home on the market to move closer to my husband's work (relieving him two hours' commute each day) while getting my kids into one of the best school districts in the state. It's symbolic of my entire 2016: I *moved* this year.

In order to do the same, you'll need to obsess over the goals you create with this workbook. If you're not actively enforcing new patterns, you will unconsciously fall into old ones. You're going to do either or.

# ⊗ THE ENTREPRENEURIAL STAGES

If you think this business feels like a roller coaster — sometimes a thrilling ride, sometimes a treacherous uphill battle, you're absolutely right. Bringing awareness to both the thrills and struggles of the ride will empower you to create results (and it's also the reason 95% will fail).

Anytime you embark on a next level leap, you'll find yourself on the following journey. I've personally been on this ride over and over again! I'm going to break it down into stages, and then I'll show you how to use this roller coaster to your advantage.

We often think of our attempts to progress as an uphill battle, but in actuality and as I'm sure you know, it's filled with peaks and crests of motivation.

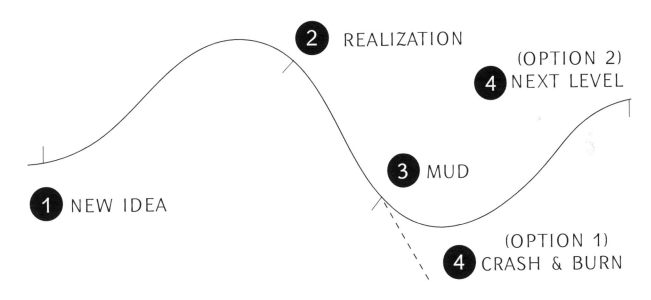

**Stage 1:** When a new idea is born and you move in its direction, there's excitement in the air. You'll likely feel like your buzzing with potential during this thrilling time and become lost in the dreamy possibilities of it all.

This stage is the one we live for as entrepreneurs. You'll jump out of bed full of energy each morning and marvel at how the hours fly by while you gather research, chart your course, and prepare for your leap to the next level.

**Stage 2:** After all of the dreaming has been arranged into a plan of action, the real work begins. This brings project realization. Hours become days that turn into weeks of work that requires real effort. It seems as though the further along your plan develops, the more effort it takes to get the job done! This stage is rough, overwhelming, and eventually becomes a real struggle. Your motivation wanes and procrastination sets in.

**Stage 3:** If you thought stage 2 was rough, buckle up for the real work. This part of the journey is why most unfinished business remains just that — unfinished.

At this stage, your enthusiasm is spent and your excitement has expired. You want to give up because the project requires enormous effort; it feels as though you're trudging through mud.

The mud is meant to be hard, and that's what makes it an easy quitting point. Most people will give up; the project will crash and burn.

However, this year you're going to push through to the finish line and beyond. To crash and burn is only an option, and it's best if we take that option off the table now. The mud is the necessary challenge that creates change. I want you to barrel through it.

**Stage 4:** When you reach the next level, it's a place of lessons learned, experience achieved, and well-deserved promotion.

This journey is a guaranteed stretch of your comfort zone. Expect everyone besides the people who love you the most to think you're crazy (and get used to it). I'm sure you can imagine the looks I get when I tell friends and extended family that I'm going to make six-figures from my home office. My business lives online, as do my colleagues and dream clients and customers. None of that makes sense to my friends and extended family because they can't see it, nor have they ever heard of such a thing before.

You see, each next step in your creative business brings you to another vulnerable bridge. Even though you've already crossed many vulnerable bridges to get to the safe and solid ground you're standing on now, the next bridge to appear on your path always presents more difficult challenges to overcome. These scary and seemingly unsafe bridges can sometimes make the journey utterly exhausting.

Worse yet, just before you take your first steps to cross the vulnerable bridge ahead of you, your mind plays tricks to protect your heart. You then desperately seek reassurance from others, and if you're anything like me, most of the people you know in the real world can't comprehend your vision, let alone the obstacles you currently face.

Sometimes the safety of your comfort zone plus fear of the unknown can stop you dead in your tracks for days, months, *even years*. And you'll get stuck there until your desire for what's on the other side of that vulnerable bridge trumps all, and you just go for it. Therein lies your challenge.

In building an online business, my comfort zone has been tested more than ever before in my life. Putting myself out there, and always in new ways, leaves me feeling vulnerable and exhausted.

**Here's an example of one of my journeys through the entrepreneurial stages:**

In 2013, I decided to launch a membership program as a way to continually follow-up with my private clients long after our one-on-one sessions had ended. I started the project with a lot of excitement in August (stage 1) with a launch deadline of October 1.

I began the project by mapping out the user experience and outlining all I wanted to include, such as courses, e-programs, video training and books. I was simultaneously working with a designer to create the logo, buttons and graphics for the club.

By early September, I was struggling to stay afloat of the workload. I realized how much was left to do, and the tasks required massive amounts of effort and energy (stage 2). This project eclipsed my regular tasks (blogging, emailing, etc.) in order to meet my publicly announced launch date.

Mid-September, I realized my web host would never handle the new membership software. I switched web hosts, which was a major undertaking in itself, nearly losing my website three times. The deadline loomed, the to-do list seemed never-ending, and I wanted to throw in the towel (stage 3). I dubbed that month "weepy September" because I was prone to spontaneously sobbing in public.

My bandwidth was so full during this period that I lost memory for everything else: account information, phone numbers, and schedules escaped me. I had to write down *everything* lest I forget. I accidentally sent my checks and checkbook to school in my son's homework folder and repeatedly left unaddressed packages in the mailbox!

Things got worse before they got better. Days before the launch date, I was still writing content and finalizing the user experience. The checkout button wasn't working until three hours before the official launch time, and I finished the very last detail one minute before at 11:59 PM on September 30. My first member joined one minute later (stage 4).

In the mud, it would have been so easy to scrap the project or delay it, to wait until I had more experience, or until I could afford to hire people with more experience, etc. But here I am, three years on the other side of it, and I can tell you it was worth every step I took in the mud. It was a necessary next level step.

## HOW TO USE THE STAGES TO YOUR ADVANTAGE

Next we're going to look at how to use the entrepreneurial stages to your advantage because you can't escape them. They're a natural, necessary part of your career.

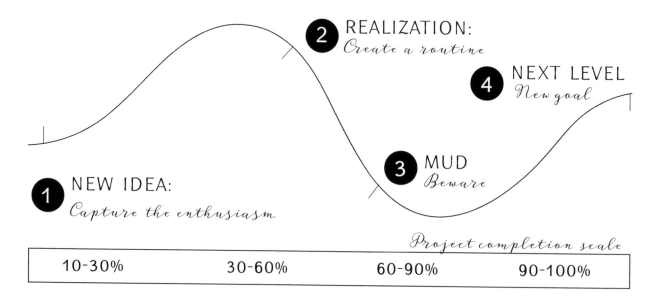

| 10-30% | 30-60% | 60-90% | 90-100% |
|--------|--------|--------|---------|

**Stage 1:** When you first discover a new idea, your enthusiasm will be highly contagious. You'll naturally want to share your excitement with anyone who will listen. Be sure to capture that energy and get your thoughts onto paper. What you write in this early stage can be channeled into sales copy, listings, descriptions, and headlines later.

The project is guaranteed to lose its luster over time. It will become a grind, and you won't be able to reproduce your "new idea" enthusiasm down the road.

Even though the new project or design is only in the beginning stages, write and record all of the public promotion now. If you're building a book or course, record the intro video and tell everyone what they're going to learn. If you're launching a new design, keep a notepad on your desk as you unpack and marvel at all the beautiful materials that you're excited to work with for the first time.

When I was working on a product-based business, I remember sitting with new-to-me gemstones and admiring them for days. I often failed to record my thoughts, and by the time the product was handmade dozens of times over, staged, photographed, and uploaded, the gemstone had simply become another product on my conveyor belt of operation. I struggled to write the listing and recapture my initial impressions.

To make the most of this stage, write blog posts and sales copy, record videos, and dictate your initial impressions. This practice will not only channel your contagious enthusiasm into useful information, but it will also remind you of the vision down the road, as you're trudging through the mud.

**Stage 2:** Maybe it's been a few days, or even a few weeks, and you've grown tired of talking about this shiny new product or design. You're ready to do the work!

Take advantage of this stage (that's still riddled with excitement) to create a routine for project completion. The work won't be difficult, you'll still be riding the momentum of your initial enthusiasm. By all means dive in, but set pace for a marathon, not a sprint.

Try not to charge full speed ahead, but rather work at a pace that keeps you always eager to get back to it. For example, the excitement of a new product might tempt you to skip meals and put in extra hours under extreme, self-imposed deadlines. Trust me, that's a recipe for disaster.

Instead, give yourself a comfortable timeline and set hours you can maintain for the duration. There are two guarantees on this roller coaster ride to the next level: Projects will always take longer than you think and the mud will always be thicker than you imagined.

**Stage 3:** Procrastination is going to tempt you now more than ever. It's going to tell you new and exciting projects are more important and more fun! Procrastination will try to convince you that maybe you need a little more research. It'll say, "Let's head to

Pinterest!" or "A new lesson from my favorite blogger? I need that before I can successfully finish this."

This is the mud. It's hard, and the only people who make it through are the people willing to go the extra mile. The project is only half-way complete at this stage, and 95% of people will quit or call it good enough. Don't be one of them.

When you begin a project, your enthusiasm will carry you on its back to the 20% completion point. It's so fun and easy — you may even be a habitual new project starter, and who could blame you? It's the best part of your job, and there's no hard work in it.

At project realization, you're near (if not past) the half-way point. By the time you get to the mud, you're incredibly close to the finish line but it's too murky to see it yet. Use this stage to your advantage by keeping the completion point front and center.

I love to map huge, daunting, mud-running, marathon-type projects into a simple bar scale so I can figure out how much further I have to go.

## FILL IN THE DISTANCE BETWEEN WHERE YOU ARE NOW & HOW FAR YOU HAVE YET TO GO (I.E. 0, 25%, 50%, ETC.)

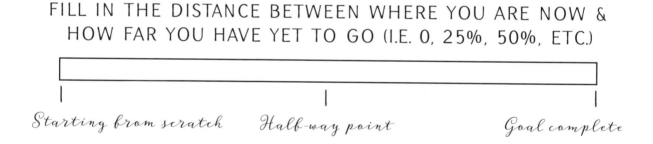

*Starting from scratch*          *Half-way point*          *Goal complete*

Would you want to run a marathon without knowing how far the finish line was? Of course not! After hours of aimless running, your morale would give out long before your body. This stage will call you to dig deep. Do your best to keep pace, and always know the remaining distance to the finish line.

**Stage 4:** Take care not to rest on your laurels once you reach the next level, thereby creating a new comfort zone. I would advise you to leave whitespace in your calendar between your next level leaps, but have your next goal ready to make the most of this stage of the ride.

When you understand the natural entrepreneurial stages, it empowers you by curing the need for instant gratification, ensuring next level success.

# *Process*

Every year on my blog, I lead a series titled *A New Year for A New You: 7 Days of Review* which includes prompts similar to the ones you're about to fill out. During the series, I offer readers a new list of review questions each day. I then blog my answers from the previous day before issuing the next set of prompts.

When I write that series, I always go back on previous years to collect questions and ideas for the current year. And a few years in, the *New Year for a New You* series was responsible for a life-changing wake-up call.

Most people don't have the advantage of reviewing their previous goals and challenges each year, but I have a 4-year public record of mine. As I reviewed past series to copy questions ("Where is time being wasted? What are your biggest challenges? What were your worst setbacks?"), I realized I might as well be copying all the answers, too!

What I planned to discuss in 2014 were the same problems I'd written in 2013. Looking back a year further, I found the same challenges, setbacks, and bad habits again! I couldn't believe my eyes … I was keeping my problems year after year.

As I read back over three years' worth of the same relationship problems, financial setbacks, weight issues, and bad habits, I got emotional. That moment still makes me tear up today. It broke my heart that I wasn't making positive changes for myself, that I was unknowingly so reluctant to make choices that would create a better life.

I've learned that we get very comfortable with our obstacles, for one reason or another:

* We like the nurturing it brings from the outside world,
* We're addicted to the dramatics an unsolved problem adds to our life, or
* **(Most likely) We feel overwhelmed, uncertain, and too scared to take the first step in the right direction.**

Is there something in your life — your weight, your health, your career, your income, your relationships — that you've been struggling with for too long?

*Are you willing to change it once and for all?*

17

*what worked this past year?*

WHAT ARE YOUR FAVORITE MEMORIES?

⏰ WHAT WAS TIME VERY WELL SPENT?

💰 WHAT WAS MONEY VERY WELL SPENT?

WHAT DID YOU ACCOMPLISH OR COMPLETE?

DID YOU MAKE ANY PROGRESS ON BIG LIFE GOALS IN 2016?

— EXAMPLE — *what worked this past year?* — WORKSHEET —

## WHAT ARE YOUR FAVORITE MEMORIES?

- San Francisco family trip
- Teaching a 3-day class on CreativeLive
- Family day at Hershey Park
- Summer at the pool
- Going to the movies
- Date nights with Jay

 ## WHAT WAS TIME VERY WELL SPENT?

- Building copywriting course
- Hooky days with each child
- Getting the house sale-ready
- Starting a bullet journal
- Studying
- One-day getaways with family

## WHAT WAS MONEY VERY WELL SPENT?

- Housecleaning crew
- Creative's assistant
- Drycleaning
- New Mac upgrades
- New sitting room for me
- Online business training
- New workout clothing
- Books for studying
- Books for leisure

## WHAT DID YOU ACCOMPLISH OR COMPLETE?

- Complete Copywriting course
- 3-day live workshop
- First hires
- Your Best Year 2017

## DID YOU MAKE ANY PROGRESS ON BIG LIFE GOALS IN 2016?

I built more assets for my business and finally found a town that suits us and provides convenience and connection in the northern Virginia area.

*what worked this past year?*

WHAT FELT SUCCESSFUL ABOUT 2016?

WHAT DID YOU LEARN ABOUT YOURSELF?

WHO NURTURED AND SUPPORTED YOU?

DID YOU OVERCOME ANY OBSTACLES?

WHO DID YOU ENJOY NURTURING AND SUPPORTING?

— EXAMPLE — *what worked this past year?* — WORKSHEET —

## WHAT FELT SUCCESSFUL ABOUT 2016?

- All the change and movement - the list is exhausting, but if we didn't like something this year, we changed it.
- Salary was much improved
- We made memories and went on new adventures as a family

## WHAT DID YOU LEARN ABOUT YOURSELF?

I learned that I have more hours in a day than I realized, and I honored how precious each and every hour is. I learned to better value my time.

## WHO NURTURED AND SUPPORTED YOU?

- Jay – all day long and in every way imaginable
- My babies – always on board and ready for adventure
- Kara & Jennie – in such unique and phenomenal ways, they've both greatly impacted my year.
- Clients & readers – I've never felt more heard and understood in my life.

## DID YOU OVERCOME ANY OBSTACLES?

Yes, I overcame all the fear and uncertainty that precedes overcoming obstacles. I now know that nothing can stop me.

## WHO DID YOU ENJOY NURTURING AND SUPPORTING?

The older I get, the more I treasure my family of six. I feel so blessed to like the people I love as much as I do. I appreciate them beyond words, and I hope to welcome great people into our circle in the coming year.

## *what didn't work this past year?*

WHAT WAS YOUR BIGGEST CHALLENGE?

WHAT WAS TIME WASTED?

WHAT WAS MONEY WASTED?

WHAT WOULD (OR WOULDN'T) YOU
CHANGE ABOUT HOW YOU HANDLED IT?

DO YOU HAVE ANY UNFINISHED BUSINESS TO ATTEND TO?

EXAMPLE——*what didn't work this past year?*——WORKSHEET

## WHAT WAS YOUR BIGGEST CHALLENGE?

Dealing with stress and anxiety. I was as anxious about the highs as I was about the lows this year. I need new ways to handle stress. I need to organize my schedule so that I can eliminate unnecessary panic once and for all.

## WHAT WOULD (OR WOULDN'T) YOU CHANGE ABOUT HOW YOU HANDLED IT?

Take immediate action on what can be changed or dealt with right away. Stop getting spun up about uncertainties or issues out of your control.

## WHAT WAS TIME WASTED?

I lost days to worry during our moving process, when all it took was a few phone calls and direct communication to figure things out.

## WHAT WAS MONEY WASTED?

I bought way more training than I had time for this year. Hoping to make good on the investments soon.

## DO YOU HAVE ANY UNFINISHED BUSINESS TO ATTEND TO?

I'm behind in my workload and out of routine on my workouts. That makes things feel unfinished, so a few productive weeks at full steam should do the trick.

23

*what didn't work this past year?*

DO YOU HAVE OUTSTANDING GOALS?

WHAT WAS YOUR WORST SETBACK?

WHAT HELD YOU BACK IN 2016?

DID YOU KEEP ANY BAD HABITS?

HOW DID YOU HOLD YOURSELF BACK?

## EXAMPLE—*what didn't work this past year?*—WORKSHEET

### DO YOU HAVE OUTSTANDING GOALS?

To lose weight. Moving combined with hectic work and life schedules has not helped my waistline. I'd like to lose ten pounds, feel stronger, and become more comfortable in my clothing.

### DID YOU KEEP ANY BAD HABITS?

Not managing stress, which goes hand-in-hand with not losing weight. Every workout I did was an immediate cure for pent-up anxiety.

### WHAT WAS YOUR WORST SETBACK?

The uncertainty that came with the moving process. I realized a few years back that there's only so much uncertainty I can handle at any given time, and selling my house without knowing where we'd live next pushed me over the edge.

### WHAT HELD YOU BACK IN 2016?

This is paradoxical to a previous answer, but the thing that held me back is that there are only so many hours in a day. I delegated a lot this year, but I'm realizing how much more I should take off my plate.

### HOW DID YOU HOLD YOURSELF BACK?

I tried to uncover every self-imposed limitation this year. I ask myself how and where I'm holding back often, and I allow myself to be more impulsive about things now I've managed to push myself forward all year.

—————————————— *time management* ——————————————

Time is the most precious resource you have on Earth, and the majority of people are burning it. Know the value in each of your 24 hours every day. Create a practice of asking yourself: If this moment were a dollar, am I investing it or burning it? Consider the following questions …

 WHAT ARE YOUR MAIN PRIORITIES?

*list them in order of importance:*

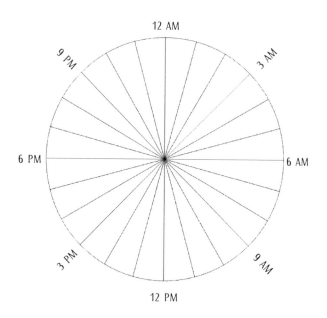

USE THE GRAPH TO CHART HOW YOU INVEST TIME DURING A TYPICAL 24-HOUR WEEKDAY.

———————————————————

DOES YOUR CHART REFLECT YOUR LIST OF PRIORITIES?
HOW MIGHT YOU REARRANGE YOUR SCHEDULE FOR BETTER RESULTS?

——— EXAMPLE ——— *time management* ——— WORKSHEET ———

## WHAT ARE YOUR MAIN PRIORITIES?

1. My family = 4 hours per day
2. My marriage = 2 hours
3. Personal wellbeing = 1 hour
4. My career = 4 hours

*8 hours sleep*

*most days = unaccounted for*

*dinner & walk with husband most nights*

*most days = unaccounted for*

*work at least 3 hours per weekday*

sleep · family · work · ?

---

### DOES YOUR CHART REFLECT YOUR LIST OF PRIORITIES?
### HOW MIGHT YOU REARRANGE YOUR SCHEDULE FOR BETTER RESULTS?

After I filled out my chart, I went back and tallied the hours I spent on each of my priorities. I feel they're pretty well reflected, except for personal wellbeing. I realized a lot of unaccounted for hours in the afternoon and evening. I would definitely benefit from a daily selfcare routine, and its clear I have time for it.

#  WHY AREN'T YOU RICH YET?

In one of my favorite books, *The Instant Millionaire: A Tale of Wisdom and Wealth* by Mark Fisher, a wise old millionaire asks a struggling young man, "How is it that you aren't rich yet? Have you ever seriously asked yourself that question?"

What an interesting perspective it brings! I love to introduce that line of questioning to any goal. Think of all the achievements you've struggled with in the past, and then ask yourself …

* Why aren't you at your ideal weight yet?
* Why haven't you reached your sales goals yet?
* Why don't you have the number of emails you want on your list yet?
* Why haven't you finished the project yet?
* Why isn't your relationship healthy yet?
* Why isn't your income what you think it should be yet?

Every obstacle in your way, every problem left unsolved, and every weakness that still needs strengthened is revealed in the answers to these questions. Let's face it, we act like spoiled children sometimes, refusing to take responsibility and rebelling against our own best intentions. It happens to us all!

Time is similar to money in that, where you spend it shows what you value most. When you know it's in your best interest to put in the work …

## WHAT DO YOU DO INSTEAD?

In other words, what's your go-to procrastination technique? Can you set it up as a reward, or is it a detrimental habit that you should stop doing altogether?

For example, I love to plan new projects. The strategy, the drawing papers, the fresh, shiny beginning stages are my favorite. When I'm procrastinating, I often play hooky on the tough work to plan my next project. It's a mental vacation from the tasks that feel like a chore, and when I give in and get lost in the new idea, it feels like I took a fun day off.

It's not a detrimental habit; I actually get things done, just not the work that needs doing. What I can do to add more creativity to the harder stages of project production is reward myself an hour a day to play and plan IF I've put in the important, deadline-oriented work in first.

If it's a detrimental and non-nutritional habit, like incessant clicking and "checking" (i.e. let me check email, let me check Instagram, let me check Facebook, let me check Pinterest, and now repeat), that needs eliminated once and for all.

At the end of the day, anybody can put off the work. Anyone can make excuses.

" YOU CANNOT DO WHAT UNSUCCESSFUL PEOPLE DO, WHICH IS TO USE ANY EXCUSE THEY CAN THINK OF TO PUT OFF THE TASKS THEY SHOULD BE COMPLETING IMMEDIATELY. INSTEAD YOU MUST ACQUIRE THE DISCIPLINE, MUSCLE MEMORY, AND ACHIEVEMENTS THAT RESULT FROM TAKING MASSIVE ACTION – WHILE OTHERS THINK, PLAN, AND PROCRASTINATE.
*– Grant Cardone, The 10x Rule*

Think of a particular struggle that's been plaguing you for entirely too long (health, income, relationships, etc.). In the next exercise, I want you to think about why you haven't achieved it, what you're doing instead, and what it will take to move the needle out of struggle and into achievement once and for all.

—————————————— *getting your goal* ——————————————

<u>THE DESIRED GOAL</u>:

HOW MANY TIMES HAVE YOU TRIED AND FAILED TO ACHIEVE THE RESULTS YOU WANT?

WHEN YOU'RE <u>NOT</u> ACTIVELY WORKING TOWARD THE GOAL, WHAT DO YOU DO INSTEAD?

APPROXIMATELY HOW LONG WOULD YOU NEED TO FOREGO THE ABOVE ACTIVITIES AND REPLACE THEM WITH A BETTER HABIT BEFORE YOU WOULD SEE RESULTS?

WHAT'S THE FIRST SMALL CHANGE YOU COULD MAKE TO YOUR SCHEDULE?

WHAT'S A REASONABLE END DATE TO ACHIEVE THE DESIRED GOAL?

I'LL START _____ AND HAVE THIS FINISHED BY _____

—— EXAMPLE —— *getting your goal* —— WORKSHEET——

THE DESIRED GOAL:  *Lose ten pounds*

HOW MANY TIMES HAVE YOU TRIED AND FAILED TO ACHIEVE THE RESULTS YOU WANT?

*Dozens, at least. I restart a program for weight loss at least every two weeks, and I fall off the wagon at every excuse.*

WHEN YOU'RE <u>NOT</u> ACTIVELY WORKING TOWARD THE GOAL, WHAT DO YOU DO INSTEAD?

*Eat without care or restriction. My activity usually stays high, but desserts, alcohol, and fast foods creep in and crash the goal.*

APPROXIMATELY HOW LONG WOULD YOU NEED TO FOREGO THE ABOVE ACTIVITIES AND REPLACE THEM WITH A BETTER HABIT BEFORE YOU WOULD SEE RESULTS?

*Four weeks would get me well underway. Eight weeks would nearly get me the goal.*

WHAT'S THE FIRST SMALL CHANGE YOU COULD MAKE TO YOUR SCHEDULE?

*I could block thirty minutes a day to either plan meals, prep meals, or do yoga (when the meals are all set).*

WHAT'S A REASONABLE END DATE TO ACHIEVE THE DESIRED GOAL?

*Three months is more than enough time to solve this issue once and for all.*

I'LL START ____*January 1*____ AND HAVE THIS FINISHED BY ___*March 30*_____

# IDENTIFY LIMITATIONS

If you find yourself saying …

* That works for [you/him/her/them], but I'm different because …
* I don't have …. [what someone else has been building for years, i.e. an email list, the traffic, the sales, the funds. etc.]
* Someone else has more [training/popularity/experience/recognition] in my space

These are justifications you're using to stay exactly where you are, snuggled in your comfort zone. Because you know as well as I do, everyone had a start somewhere.

*How are you getting in the way of your own success? What are your go-to limitations?*

For example, I wanted to create modern email opt-in landing pages for my blog, and I wanted to use the program called LeadPages to do it. It was an overwhelming obstacle I chased in my mind for months.

My limitations were that it cost money to sign up, and I didn't know how to design a landing page or work the program. After I hurdled those issues, it would take time to build the pages; they'd need copywriting, graphics, email integration, etc.

When I catch myself him-hawing over humps like these in business, I stop to assess the issue using the worksheet on the following page. I find that I've typically done nothing to conquer the issue besides fuss over it.

Then, I make a simple task list like so:

1. Decide which offer to promote on the landing page
2. Prepare that document
3. Sign up for LeadPages
4. Build the first opt-in offer
5. Promote that page

Once I finally simplify the process, the goal (that has often been on my to-do list for months) is complete within a matter of hours. You don't need to know exactly *how to do* something before you start, but you do need to start.

*do what scares you*

WHAT IS SOMETHING YOU COULD DO TO EXPAND YOUR BUSINESS, BUT YOU'VE BEEN TOO AFRAID TO TACKLE?

HAVE YOU EVER ATTEMPTED TO ACCOMPLISH THIS GOAL?

WHAT ARE THE ACTUAL COSTS OF THIS OBSTACLE?

WHAT'S STOPPING YOU FROM GOING FOR IT RIGHT NOW?

WHAT IF YOU FAILED? WHAT'S THE WORST-CASE SCENARIO?

WHAT IF YOU SUCCEEDED? WHAT'S THE BEST-CASE SCENARIO?

IS IT WORTH IT TO TRY?

#  THE SECRET TO GAINING EXPOSURE

Exposure is a vulnerable thing. If you let everyone know what you're doing, they'll know if you fail ... and that can be very scary. Right? I'm sure you've felt vulnerable about your work at some point. I imagine you know how difficult "putting yourself out there" can be. We all can relate to the fear and hesitation that occurs when you set out to do something you've never done before.

I looked up the definition of "vulnerable,"[1] and these were the options:

1. capable of or susceptible to being wounded or hurt, as by a weapon
2. open to moral attack, criticism, temptation, etc.
3. (of a place) open to assault; difficult to defend

I thought these were each so interesting, but one stood out to me more than any other: "(of a place) open to assault; difficult to defend." The dictionary used "a vulnerable bridge" as an example of the definition. It got me to thinking.

**Does a successful online business simply mean crossing the vulnerable bridge between where you are and where you want to be?**

And if so, no wonder we build armor around our dreams. Which by the way, is what I used to think I had to do in order to succeed in my creative career. I'm always taking a leap that no one I know has ever taken before, so each time I share my big dreams, they seem open to assault and difficult to defend. But, it doesn't have to be so scary.

There are three steps to mastering exposure: (1.) Get comfortable with exposure; (2.) Get comfortable asking for exposure; and (3.) Ask for exposure all the time. Let's discuss.

**#1 Get comfortable with exposure.**

It took me over a year to tell anyone I knew personally that I was in business.
The truth is, I was scared of what a few skeptical friends and family might think of the whole idea. I soon realized that I was waiting for my big break before I shared the news. I wanted something to validate me, to make my business seem worthy and established.

---

[1] HTTP://WWW.DICTIONARY.COM/BROWSE/VULNERABLE

After the first year of business, I decided NO MORE HOLDING BACK. I realized that the people who are doing all the succeeding in life are the people who *take chances* and *leap on faith*. I realized the people in my life should build me up, and I was no longer going to settle for anything less. I became vulnerable and open for all the world to see.

Since then, I've absolutely made mistakes. I've wept at rejection. I've put things out into the world that nobody had any interest in. I've lost a lot of money and wasted a lot of resources. Do you think me a failure? Of course not! You rack it all up to lessons learned and experience gained!

To have a thriving small business, you have to own it! You have to tell all your friends about it, and let your passion escape you wherever you go.

#2  **Get comfortable asking for exposure.**

The way I see it, you're going to ASK somebody for something to get this thing you're doing off the ground. You're either going to ASK the customer to buy in, or you're going to ASK yourself and/or your family to justify this expensive hobby you have.

#3 **Ask for exposure all the time.**

I have spent the last six years asking myself and anybody who might give me a little bit of insight: *Who else would "get" what I do? Who would appreciate my product?* And then, I make a point to send my message in that direction.

This is how I approach gaining exposure for my business. I send bottles out into the ocean everyday; it's become second nature. My comfort zone has become more of an uncomfortable zone.

## WHAT IS YOUR BIGGEST OBSTACLE?

In regards to exposure, what is your biggest obstacle? Is it not knowing any other people who do what you do for a living? Are you still waiting for sales? Validation? A big break? Does "go big" or "get seen" go against the grain of your personality? Is there some further training or experience you think you need in order to be taken seriously?

# IF I KNEW I COULD NOT FAIL

Limitations and exposure are the perfect segue to the next chapter; words cannot how powerful and freeing this exercise can be. It's time to think up the wildest, most amazing dreams imaginable.

In 2014, I published a blog post that would change my career forever. It was titled, *If I Knew I Could Not Fail, I Would …* in which I listed all of the things I would do right now if I knew I could not fail. It challenged me to defy self-imposed limitations and dream without fear.

I wrote down everything I could think of to finish the sentence, "If I knew I could not fail, I would …" My answers were as follows:

1.   Focus all of my efforts on group coaching
2.   Lead live, in-person workshops for groups of 100+
3.   Host a women's retreat for 20 creatives
4.   Start a podcast

So why hadn't I gone for these big dreams? I guess I was just … scared? Waiting for permission? Hoping to be recognized, validated, or sponsored? Looking for a big break? And that's exactly what I coach my clients not to do. I certainly could not leave my career wish list hanging. It was time for me to cross these vulnerable bridges.

I got straight to work on the one I wanted most: I planned a women's retreat alongside an amazing line-up of inspirational leaders in my field. In February 2015, I co-hosted an intimate retreat in a luxurious, oceanfront home in Charleston, South Carolina.

It answered a craving I didn't even realize I was having; I longed for a deeper connection, and the creative retreat — where I was able to meet people face-to-face, look into their eyes, and feel the magic in the room — was only the beginning.

Truth be told, this work-at-home business can be lonely. My "If I Knew I Could Not Fail" list showed me how much I missed building, brainstorming, troubleshooting, and goofing off with co-workers *in real life.* I missed the bonds that come from working partnerships. In addition to the retreat, I created an online membership program, The Luminaries Club, and have repeatedly taught to thousands of students during live broadcasts on CreativeLive.

*vulnerable bridges*

Say the following prompt out loud, and fearlessly record whatever comes to you.

IF I KNEW I COULD NOT FAIL, I WOULD …

" THERE IS FREEDOM WAITING FOR YOU, ON THE BREEZES OF THE SKY, AND YOU ASK,
'WHAT IF I FAIL?'

OH BUT MY DARLING, WHAT IF YOU FLY?     *— Erin Hanson*

WHAT AM I TRULY CRAVING?

# Prepare

In order to create change, you have to make the tough choices. There's no simpler way to put this. My goal for this section is to prepare you for, not only the success, but also the struggle ahead.

By January 15, 95% of people who set New Year resolutions will have already given up on them. That's a heartbreaking realization; the majority quit on themselves in only two weeks! I don't want you to be among them. Instead, you'll be one of the 5% who actually achieves the goals they set for themselves.

The reason most people miss the mark is very simple: Change is hard. Before you reap the rewards, you have to crawl through a slew of challenging obstacles and emotions. I won't sugarcoat this for you; I want you to be prepared.

Prepare to face uncertainty and stare down your biggest fears. Prepare to do your best work without guaranteed results or fanfare. Prepare to face negativity, frustration, and criticism. Prepare to confuse and baffle; most people will have long given up while you continue to persist.

The extreme minority insist on solving their problems rather than adapting to them. Five percent of people in this world …

* Achieve extreme wealth
* Operate successful businesses
* Take their career to the highest level
* Create exceptional health and fitness habits
* Nurture clean and loving relationships
* Strengthen their spiritual and mental weaknesses

If any of these things were easy to achieve, everyone would have them. Prepare yourself now: your goals are out there, like a destination on a map, awaiting your arrival.

To truly make it happen this year, you must be willing to embark on the journey that everyone else makes excuses to avoid. You will experience negative feelings along the way. They're quite natural. They are part of the process; trust that they will get easier to endure. This book is designed to help you overcome them!

I felt very called to share my journey to a six-figure salary this year, even though money conversations make people very uncomfortable, or worse, money conversations make people compare.

If you want to compare anything, compare where you're at now to the income reports I shared on my blog in 2014. I knew how to make one figure very well, and I made it without fail — nothing more, nothing less. That was the year that I felt stalled and unsure, and the struggle was real. Making tens of thousands of dollars a month is surreal, and the funniest part about it is …

*Everyone wants my business today! The vision is alive, and so they believe!*

Nobody wanted my business in years one through four when I worked just as hard, scraping by, frustrated and ready to quit, but I refused to quit because *I believed* and *my husband and children believed* in my calling and my message and my purpose.

For years, I wrote down six-figure goals and then repeated the work that guaranteed I'd make much less. It was a case of doing the same things, but expecting different results. Trust me, that strategy doesn't work!

If you don't completely rearrange your routine so that it's relentlessly barreling toward the new destination, you'll end up not much farther from where you left off. You need to fiercely believe in the new destination and take steps closer to it every day.

**Therefore, and as a general rule of thumb:** If you think you might be too obsessed about your goals, obsess more!

At the start of the year, I'm so hyped up about my goals that it's all I can talk about! Just ask my husband! When I started out in 2015 with the system laid out for you in this workbook, I couldn't help but wonder: *Was I spending too much time thinking about my goals and not enough time moving toward them? Should I do less obsessing and take more action?* If you're doing it right, you'll wonder the same.

In 2015, I set out to shatter my income ceiling once and for all. When I doubted myself and stopped obsessing about my goals, I was back to the old way of doing things (that created the same income I'd made for years) within 10 days.

Never stop obsessing about the goal.

" HIGH-PERFORMING PEOPLE SET GOALS RELIGIOUSLY AND TRACK THEM RELIGIOUSLY. THEY OBSESS ABOUT WHETHER THEY'RE HITTING OR MISSING THOSE GOALS, AND WHY. IF YOU DON'T SET AND TRACK GOALS, LIFE JUST PASSES YOU BY. *– Cameron Herald*

Along the way, if a goal feels insurmountable, stop and question WHY. If you would like to triple your sales or meet a certain income goal, but it makes you feel anxious just recording such a gigantic ask, figure out what specifically is so scary about it.

This year, six-figures was the destination and I was barreling toward it. Nothing could stop me. I'd never been there before, but I refused to fall short. If I feared not meeting the goal, or if I was tempted to reduce it, I questioned WHY: Don't feel worthy? Afraid to ask for sales? Making excuses to keep doing only what you know?

When you really want something, nothing can stand in your way. I know you know this about yourself, too. That's why I'm currently obsessed with boxing movies: Rocky, Southpaw, Creed, etc. If you're ready to conquer the year, I highly recommend them.

What I notice is that every strong fighter always has a culmination of four things: determination, discipline, a timeline, and a trainer.

It's the winning formula. The boxer always comes in determined to do whatever it takes to achieve their goal. He exhibits extreme self-discipline, focusing his efforts solely and specifically on the goal he's trying to achieve. He has a timeline to train to his very best fighting condition within a specific deadline (the fight date). Finally, he has a trainer in the corner who keeps him on track - whose only job is to keep the fighter's eye on the prize.

Let's apply this winning formula to your business. I know you have the determination. I trust you're building your discipline every day. Your timeline is 12-months, but you're encouraged to book smaller fights (deadlines) within that period. And last but not least, this workbook is your trainer.

It sounds so simple, yet it's life's greatest challenge. The question is: How good can you stand it? And, are you ready to train for it? Are you willing to put in the hard work that will get the goal?

# WHAT TO FOCUS ON

Too often you get caught up in doing for doing's sake in online business. You might make products even though your current inventory's not moving (making for making's sake), post status updates online even though what you're saying isn't connecting (marketing for marketing's sake), email because you know you're supposed to (emailing for emailing's sake), and research everything you can find online to try to make what isn't working *work already* (training for training's sake).

You probably find yourself getting swept away by a lot of business-building ideas that don't even make sense: such as, "Open another storefront" (when you already have one storefront that's not selling), or "Grow my account on Twitter" (when none of your customers/clients even use that platform), or "Start Periscoping" (because it's the latest random advice floating around *all of the other* social platforms that day).

*None of it matters.* It's all doing for doing's sake. You don't need two storefronts anymore than I need two blogs! It will only create more things that don't matter to fuss over. It's scrambling, and you're better than that! Your work deserves more attention, your time is extremely valuable, and your business is meant to give back!

**To grow a successful online business you need:** (1.) A website that attracts and converts, (2.) A marketing strategy that wins, and (3.) A plan to optimize numbers one and two.

Therefore, don't open more storefronts if the original site isn't working. Instead, spend your time and energy improving your existing storefront! Don't open new social media accounts if you're not connecting with the profiles you already have. Instead, study the platform with the most potential to grow your following through the roof!

If you're in online business, you've likely heard of the Pareto principle (aka the 80/20 rule) which states that (from Wikipedia), "For many events, roughly 80% of the effects come from 20% of the causes." For example — and those of you who have an email list will know this to be true, 80% of your revenue comes from 20% of your customers.

The reason this rule is examined in the online world is because it's a hack for doing more of what matters to your bottom line. If 20% of your working hours produce 80% of your results, then that means that the other 80% of the time you spend produces only 20% of your desired results. How would your results improve if you focused all of your attention on the 20% of work that adds to 80% of your bottom line? That's what we're going to explore in this section.

Ask yourself the following questions to find out which 20% of your applied efforts are producing 80% of your desired results:

---

## WHAT WAS YOUR BEST BUSINESS PAYDAY OF ALL TIME?

---

## WHERE DO YOU INVEST ENERGY WITHOUT RETURN?

---

Where you spend your working hours should always result in one of two things:

1.  Growth (*Will it attract email subscribers and traffic?*), and/or
2.  Profit (*Will it make money for my business?*)

If it doesn't result in either of those things (meaning, you're fussing, checking, or otherwise doing for doing's sake), it's not helping your business' bottom line. When you write a list of tasks you need to do for your business, always ask: **To what end?**

* To what end are you building another website?
* To what end are you blogging?
* To what end are you making more listings?
* To what end are you tweaking your branding?
* To what end are you creating a new social media account?
* To what end are you emailing?

#  TRUST THE BUSINESS TO PROVIDE

Two of the toughest questions I answered in 2016 were:

* Do you trust your business to provide?
* Do you trust yourself to follow through on what's required?

I've already mentioned that I broke the six-figure barrier this year, but here's what you don't know: A few months before the money came in, I made a firm decision to trust my business and better value my own services.

I started to operate as though I were already running a six-figure business. I stopped him-hawing on trivial decisions in both personal life and work, such as, *Should I buy that book? Should I upgrade my phone? Should I invest in more business training?*

Many of us are so afraid of expenses — we look at upgrades as a direct loss. It's only during the decision-making process that it feels that way; as soon as you make the decision, you instantly feel richer and do better. This is true for both personal and professional aspects, in fact, they often intertwine.

For example, I chased the same financial issue in my mind for years. My eldest daughter was self-conscious about her smile; the older she got, the more crooked her front teeth became. I had a good idea of how much braces cost, but there were always bills or other financial priorities in the way.

Around the time I was upgrading my business (and after two years of fussing over the cost of orthodontic care), I booked an appointment. I wasn't sure how I was going to pay for the braces, but I took my daughter in for a consultation anyway.

At the consultation, I immediately agreed to the cost and terms of service. I decided that I was done chasing this problem; I was just going to solve it. My daughter exploded into happy tears as I filled out the final paperwork.

And then, the most magical thing happened. I made enough to cover the entire bill within two weeks of signing the contract. She hadn't even started treatment, yet I had paid her account in full.

The moral of the story: I finally trusted my business to provide, and so it did.

*building trust*

WHAT DECISION HAVE YOU BEEN HIM-HAWING ABOUT, CHASING ON AND ON FOR ABSOLUTELY NO REASON? WHAT ARE YOU HOLDING YOURSELF BACK FROM UPGRADING?

IN WHAT AREAS ARE YOU FAILING TO TRUST YOUR BUSINESS TO PROVIDE?

WHAT'S THE FIRST STEP, CALL, OR CONSULTATION YOU CAN MAKE TOWARD YOUR UPGRADE?

There's a floodgate of abundance behind these obstacles. Make the decision to remove your blocks this year, and allow your business provide!

# YOUR INCOME GOAL

The next worksheet is specifically designed to help you figure out how much money you want to spend on your business and what you'd like your salary to be.

Surprise expenses are never a good idea, and an equally anxiety-inducing situation is to have a looming expense that you know you should take care of, but you procrastinate on taking the plunge. This exercise is not meant to stress you out; it's here to help you get all of those upcoming expenses out of your head and onto the page where you can begin to deal with them.

I'm also going to encourage you to make 2017 the year you stop jerry-rigging your business once and for all. Online entrepreneurs have a tendency to "make do" with their operation while waiting for it to make larger amounts of money, so that they can afford to stop making do with their operation!

I finally realized that if I want to earn upwards of 100K, I need a 100K plan combined with a 100K mindset. I need to make 100K decisions. It'll require a 100K work ethic. And most of all, I need to believe my business is worth every single dollar now!

I bought the training I needed, upgraded to the software I wanted, and I hired help. My business wasn't earning six-figures at the time, but I stopped looking at investments as losses and started trusting their return.

**That part's important:** I trusted my business to provide, and so it finally did. I know how stressful business expenses can be. I never mean to make the leap look easy, but … it was. In fact, leaping is a lot easier than standing on the edge thinking about the leap.

Come to this exercise knowing how much you currently pay yourself, what you'd like to invest in your business in the coming year, along with its existing operating expenses.

You'll learn the <u>required minimum</u> your business needs to make in order to operate successfully. That's your new quota; don't allow your income to fall below this figure each month. Then, I'll show you how to aim for the <u>advantage income goal</u>. It's the trick to breaking the "nothing more, nothing less" pattern. It will challenge you to stretch yourself beyond the figures you believe you can make.

## income goal

CURRENT ANNUAL OPERATING EXPENSES -

DESIRED RESERVE (BUSINESS SAVINGS) -

MUST-HAVE UPGRADES AND SUPPORT -

REQUIRED MINIMUM =

WISH LIST BUSINESS UPGRADES AND SUPPORT -

WISH LIST NEEDS -

ADVANTAGE TOTAL =

CURRENT SALARY -

MUST-HAVE LIFE UPGRADES -

FAMILY NEEDS -

PERSONAL NEEDS -

REQUIRED MINIMUM -

WISH LIST LIFE UPGRADES AND SUPPORT -

WISH LIST NEEDS -

ADVANTAGE TOTAL -

EXPENSE REQUIRED MINIMUM + SALARY REQUIRED MINIMUM:  /12 MONTHS=

EXPENSE ADVANTAGE TOTAL + SALARY ADVANTAGE TOTAL:  /12 MONTHS=

—— EXAMPLE —————— *income goal* —————— WORKSHEET ——

CURRENT ANNUAL OPERATING EXPENSES - *$10k*

DESIRED RESERVE (BUSINESS SAVINGS) - *$1k*

MUST-HAVE UPGRADES AND SUPPORT - *part-time assistant – $20k per year*
*accountant – $1k, cleaning crew – $3k*

REQUIRED MINIMUM = *$34k*

WISH LIST BUSINESS UPGRADES AND SUPPORT - *videographer – $8k,*
*photographer – $2k*

WISH LIST NEEDS - *branding – $5k,*
*web development – $5k*

*required + wish list*

ADVANTAGE TOTAL = *$54k*

CURRENT SALARY - *$72k*

MUST-HAVE LIFE UPGRADES - *regular mini-getaways – $5k*

FAMILY NEEDS - *dental and orthodontic care – $5k*

PERSONAL NEEDS - *selfcare (hair, spa, gym, etc.) – $2k*

REQUIRED MINIMUM - *$84k*

WISH LIST LIFE UPGRADES AND SUPPORT - *painters – $3k, dry-cleaning – $1k*

WISH LIST NEEDS - *home updates – $20k*

*required + wish list*

ADVANTAGE TOTAL - *$105k*

EXPENSE REQUIRED MINIMUM + SALARY REQUIRED MINIMUM: *$118k* /12 MONTHS= *$9,800/mo.*

EXPENSE ADVANTAGE TOTAL + SALARY ADVANTAGE TOTAL: *$159k* /12 MONTHS= *$12,200/mo.*

# BUILD AN ANNUAL STRATEGY

*Your Best Year* plan is designed around the upcoming calendar year and your business' strongest season. This strategy enables you to keep your priorities in order of importance: Your life *then* your business. It will not only help you eliminate the scramble, it also guarantees you'll improve your results and enhance your career.

**First, look at the coming year and identify where you'll need time off**, such as summer vacation, winter holidays, important dates, back to school, etc. List these special events on your calendar *before* listing business-related projects or promotions.

**In the example exercise, I've noted all of my personal time with a star.***

| JANUARY | FEBRUARY | MARCH | APRIL |
|---|---|---|---|
| | ★ *weekend break* | | |

| MAY | JUNE | JULY | AUGUST |
|---|---|---|---|
| | ★ *summer break* | ★ *vacation* | ★ *back to school* |

| SEPTEMBER | OCTOBER | NOVEMBER | DECEMBER |
|---|---|---|---|
| | ★ *weekend break* | | ★ *downtime* |

I'm not out of the game / not working when you see personal notations, but it's important to bring awareness to the events to ensure I leave plenty of space for them.

For example, I tend to go stir-crazy in February, and it messes with my emotions and my outlook. I made note to plan a long weekend away that month. I like to spend a lot of time with my children during summer break, so I made note of when school's out and back in session. I love to take December at a slower pace so that I can shop at leisure and bake for days without worrying about my schedule.

Notice that these personal occasions are on the calendar long before any product or promotional launches, and you can see my year already starting to take shape. I'm obviously not going to launch a new course or host a busy promotion in December (or worse, as a last-minute scramble for business) because I've already claimed white space in my calendar that month. I can set up the rest of the year to ensure I get time off.

I'm always looking for ways to improve my work - life flow. When I notice something I love or dislike about my schedule, I take note. Some examples are:

* I dislike projects that drag on for longer than three months
* I'm desperately craving a retreat/getaway at this time
* I'd like to purely focus on the family during this holiday or occasion
* Take a personal day once a month

Strive to constantly gain more intel on your routine and schedule. The creative energy you spend in this business is an expensive fuel to burn. If you don't bring awareness to and continually replenish that energy, you'll quickly gas out and fail to meet your goals.

**The next thing you're going to add to your calendar is your busier seasons.** If you have an existing business, you can check your annual statistics for the months where you get most traffic. If not, you can use my examples as a guide.

It is the nature of business to have hot and cold seasons, most do. This technique is in place to help you utilize those seasons to their fullest. For example, it seems like everyone is on the internet in January, whereas in February, nobody's online. There will be plenty of average months in between, but it's important to take note of the high and low tides in particular. **I've noted seasons with a bullet.**

| JANUARY | FEBRUARY | MARCH | APRIL |
|---|---|---|---|
| *everybody > internet* •• | *weekend break* <br> *nobody > internet* • | | *nobody > internet* • |

| MAY | JUNE | JULY | AUGUST |
|---|---|---|---|
| | ★ *summer break* | ★ *vacation* | ★ *back to school* |

| SEPTEMBER | OCTOBER | NOVEMBER | DECEMBER |
|---|---|---|---|
| | ★ *weekend break* | *everybody > internet* • | ★ *downtime* |

# $ MONEY MAKERS

With full awareness of your personal schedule, as well as busy and slow seasons, it's time to plug in the <u>money makers</u>. There are many different ways your business can earn money, but I'm going to advise you to specifically name three to six money makers. These will be the larger promotions or projects that anchor your entire year.

When scheduling your money makers, you're going to naturally avoid the slow seasons and steer clear of your personal occasions. **Here's an example of a service-based business (my blog is the point of sale). Money makers are noted with an arrow.**➔

JANUARY
*everybody > internet* ••
➔ *Shop 2.0 course*

FEBRUARY
*weekend break*
*nobody > internet* •

MARCH
➔ *new book*

APRIL
*nobody > internet* •

MAY
➔ *Copy course*

JUNE
★ *summer break*

JULY
★ *vacation*

AUGUST
★ *back to school*

SEPTEMBER

OCTOBER
★ *weekend break*
*Your Best Year*

NOVEMBER
*everybody > internet* •

DECEMBER
★ *downtime*

**Here's an example of a product-based business (a storefront is the point of sale).**

JANUARY
*everybody > internet* ••
➔ *New Year special*

FEBRUARY
*weekend break*
*nobody > internet* •

MARCH
➔ *spring launch*

APRIL
*nobody > internet* •

MAY
➔ *semi-annual sale*

JUNE
★ *summer break*

JULY
★ *vacation*

AUGUST
★ *back to school*

SEPTEMBER
➔ *fall launch*

OCTOBER
★ *weekend break*

NOVEMBER
*everybody > internet* •
➔ *semi-annual*

DECEMBER
★ *downtime*
➔ *free shipping*

So much is revealed when big projects are added to the annual calendar. Now you know when you need to be working on what. Rather than be stifled by the slow seasons, you can use them to your advantage. You can start prepping, promoting, and creating excitement around the next big event. You can make your best seasons even better. With this big picture in mind, you will know when your efforts will be rewarded.

This calendar will also help you to determine when to stock up on inventory, when to work ahead, when to take a break, and so on and so forth. *Your Best Year* is designed to help you pinpoint *what* to work on, this calendar helps you define *when*.

Your business rises and falls according to the effort you invest. When you know your seasons, you can create your own peaks and crest rather than become victim to them.

Use the form below to plug in your personal time, seasonal tides, and money makers.

# YOUR ANNUAL STRATEGY

| JANUARY | FEBRUARY | MARCH | APRIL |
|---------|----------|-------|-------|

| MAY | JUNE | JULY | AUGUST |
|-----|------|------|--------|

| SEPTEMBER | OCTOBER | NOVEMBER | DECEMBER |
|-----------|---------|----------|----------|

# YOUR BEST YEAR PLAN

As I mentioned in the opening, I did four specific things to exceed my goals and shatter my income ceilings this year. I made …

* My goals resolute
* My strategies specific
* My system efficient
* My action plan productive

In this section, I'm going to show you how to do the same. First, let's cover some fundamental principles of goal-setting.

## YOUR GOAL

Your goal should be your business manager. In other words, you should always be reporting to it. Gauge your success by whether or not you're meeting its expectations. Your goal is counting on you to get the job done.

Your goal should always result in growth or profit, and preferably both. One usually feeds the other: Growth brings more profit, and more profit brings faster growth.

Your goal should be a game-changer, something that's guaranteed to take you to the next level of your career. It should test your boundaries and stretch your comfort zone. Some examples are:

* Build my email list to 12,000 subscribers, tripling its current size (growth)
* Earn $102,000 in 2017, doubling my previous year's salary (profit)

In my early days, I spent entire years focused on growth. I looked at the start-up of my online business as though I were building a portfolio for my clients. I spent the majority of my days blogging, mentoring for free, and creating a library of opt-ins.

Now that I have a substantial foundation in business, I shift my focus between growth and profit. I prefer to set income goals because it's an umbrella to all strategies, as you'll see in the upcoming examples.

Next I'll cover strategies, systems, and action plans, but keep in mind that you will always work backward from the year's main goal.

**Remember the daily scramble?** A typical online business strategy looks like this …

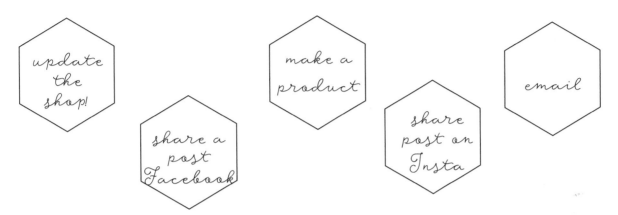

With this *Your Best Year* plan, you'll never wonder what you should be working on again. Here's a look at the complete system …

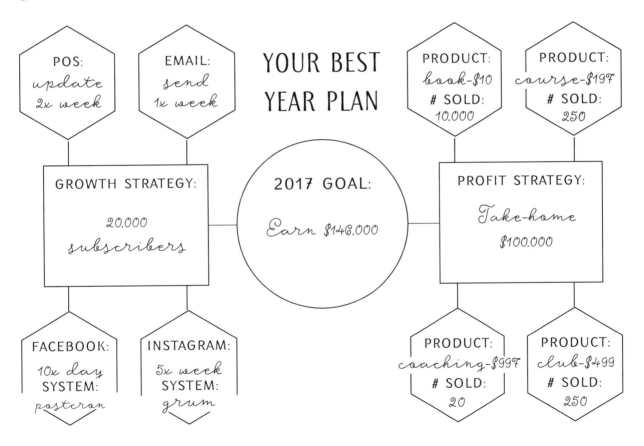

See the difference?

In the first graphic, tactics are being misfired as strategies, each one only answering its own purpose (aka, doing for doing's sake). The activities aren't connected to each other, and they won't result in significant progress.

In the second graphic, every activity has a purpose. Every money maker has a target. Notice how smaller activities always funnel into a larger strategy, they're systemized where possible, and each one ultimately feeds the goal.

To compare these two approaches in business to physically reaching a destination, it would be like …

(1.) Leaving your house with no destination in mind, making a series of random left and right turns as you go, and aimlessly driving in circles until you run out of gas **versus …**

(2.) Leaving your house with a destination in mind, a timeline for getting there, and a GPS to guide you.

**Instead, begin to ask: Does this activity feed my goal?**

For example, my big goal for 2016 was to welcome 500 members to my membership program, The Luminaries Club. I knew that 500 members would enable me to hire club counselors, create an ongoing support system, and have more time to make valuable educational tools and resources.

Therefore, I questioned everything on my to-do list as to whether or not it would help me reach that goal.

Will checking Facebook or Twitter 23 time a day help me welcome 500 new members? Absolutely not. That's why I'm rarely there anymore. Will Pinterest help me welcome 500 new members? A little bit. I give it about 20 minutes per day. Will writing an epic blog post that gets pinned 1,000 times help me to achieve my goal? You know it. That's the work I need to focus on!

Anytime you start fussing over your schedule or looming to-do list, I want you to question what you're doing, and more importantly, WHY you're doing it.

# THE STRATEGIES

Once you have a goal in place (and it's both resolute and firm), it's time to develop the strategies that will help you achieve it. The strategies are divided into our two main categories: growth and profit.

Your growth strategy consists of all the places you build and market your business online: your website or storefront (POS = point of sale), your email list, and two to three social media platforms where you reach and connect with your ideal customers. The systems you use are what automates as much of these activities as possible, such as Postcron (a social media scheduler) or Grum (an Instagram scheduler).

Your profit strategy consists of the money makers (three to six annual products or promotions) you named in the previous chapter. The number of products sold for any launch or promotion is a target for how much money could potentially be earned.

Let's look at my example graphic again, paying attention to where these take effect …

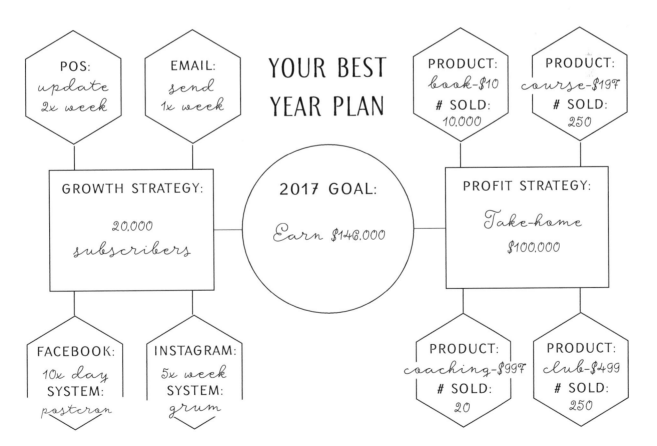

# THE ACTION PLAN

We want your action plan to be as productive as possible, so before I send you off to create your own *Your Best Year* plan, let's assess your current operation.

Keeping your goal for 2017 front and center, ask yourself what activities you're willing to commit to all year in order to achieve it. Your challenge is going to be to continuously move the needle toward progress even when you're not getting immediate results. Remember, each small step gets you closer to the destination.

The real secret to success is persistence. You must keep trudging along even when it feels like nobody's buying, listening, reading, caring, supporting, or sharing.

Are you willing to go the next 12 months at full speed toward your desired results? The months are going to pass no matter what, so what are you going to make of them?

**Let's start with your growth strategy.** These questions will help you fill out *Your Best Year* plan on the following page.

How often will you update your point of sale? This is the website or storefront where you offer your product, and the hub of your online business. Your point of sale could be the blog where you offer digital products, your Etsy storefront where you offer a handmade product, or the website that houses something similar. At what frequency will you commit to freshen that site with new products, blog posts, or information?

How often will you email your list? There's no "one size fits all" to any of these questions, especially this one. I email my blog readers an average of once per week, but I only emailed my product-based business an average eight times per year. It doesn't matter the frequency you choose, but do commit to a routine.

What social media platforms do you not only reach out, but also connect and engage with followers? Most successful online business owners dominate one or two social media platforms (*not all*). I advise my clients to avoid being everywhere, connecting with no one. Instead, pick your three most successful platforms and focus on enhancing your presence there.

Finally, how can you make your operation more efficient? Look for systems that will automate your workflow so you don't have to touch or "check it" everyday. Which tasks can be batched, scheduled ahead, or outsourced?

Your growth strategy will require time, training, practice, patience, and small investments in scheduling software, but it will all pay off exponentially.

**Next, look at your profit strategy.** This consists of products or promotions (your three to six money makers) for the year. You want to list each money maker, how much you'll charge (or average sale amount , if it's a product promotion), and then write a target for how much money could potentially be earned.

This will help you project whether or not the money makers will add up to the desired income goal, after taxes and expenses are deducted.

On your worksheet, you'll also be prompted to name the date of release. I like to spread my major promotions out, leaving eight to twelve weeks between the next big sale. Here again, there's no "one size fits all". You know the seasons of your business better than anyone.

Your profit strategy requires traffic (online visitors), planning, training, copywriting, marketing, and later, an investment in advertising. Because once you have a working system in place, more traffic is the easiest part! Traffic is for sale; you can buy it at anytime.

This plan ensures that each activity feeds the goal and keeps your operation running like a well-oiled machine. It's time to build *Your Best Year* plan.

*your best year plan*

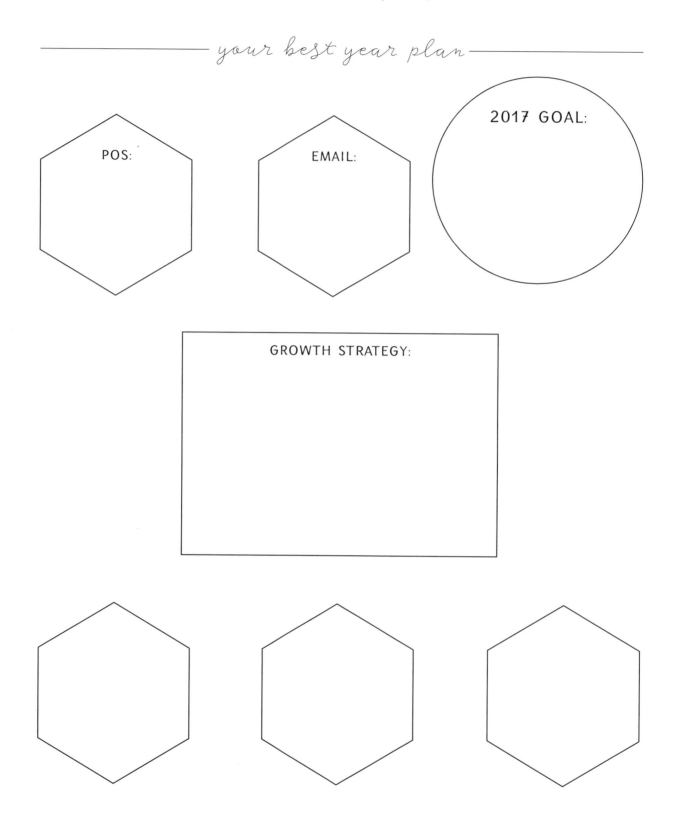

POS:

EMAIL:

2017 GOAL:

GROWTH STRATEGY:

*social media + systems*

*your best year plan*

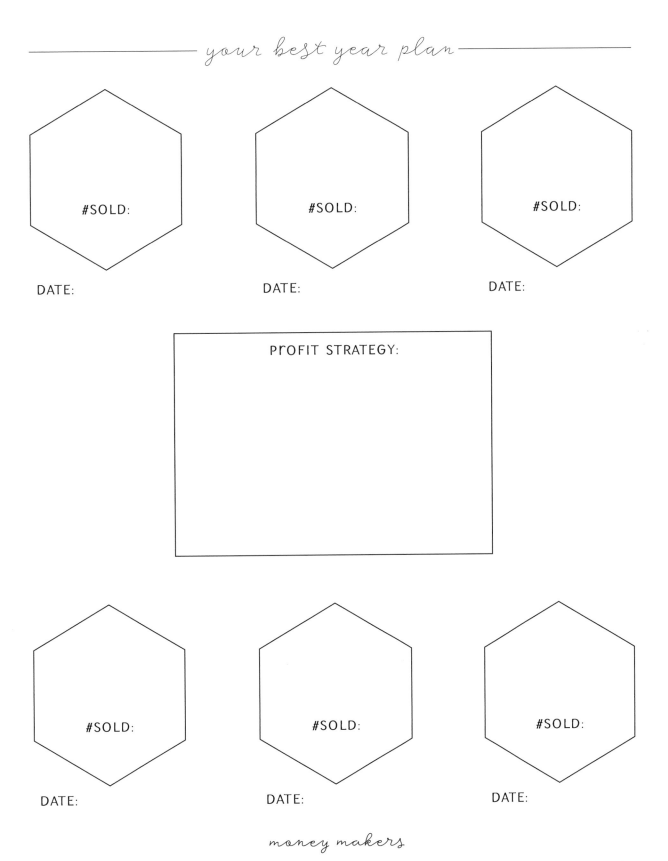

#SOLD:

DATE:

#SOLD:

DATE:

#SOLD:

DATE:

PROFIT STRATEGY:

#SOLD:

DATE:

#SOLD:

DATE:

#SOLD:

DATE:

*money makers*

# *Practice*

" PRACTICE | NOUN | PRAC·TICE :
THE ACTUAL USE OF AN IDEA AS OPPOSED TO THEORIES ABOUT SUCH USE. *– Google*

For most online business owners, the way we feel about business is its measuring stick for success. And don't forget, we're always resetting our zeros.

For example, I remember the days when I dreamt of having 1,000 subscribers on my email list. I visualized how successful I would feel to have that many people so eager to hear about my updates and promotions. Not surprisingly, that number came and went without notice. At around 850 subscribers my sights were set on 5,000 subscribers. Before I'd even reached it, 1,000 subscribers became my new zero.

It's time to break that pattern once and for all. You are going to organize annual objectives into quarterly progress logs, monthly priorities, weekly task lists, and daily activities. You'll also schedule regular review and find new ways to improve your work-life balance throughout the year. Let this section of the workbook be your measuring stick for success; it's a non-biased, non-emotional look at the big picture.

First, let's talk long-term goals. Typical life and business advice will tell you to make a 6-month, 1-year, 5-year and 10-year plan. That's just never worked for me. Why? Because I don't have a traditional career with a foreseeable trajectory. I've chased big dreams because it seemed like what I was supposed to do next, only to find out that I hated the work! That throws most conventional 10-year plans out the window.

## THE POWER OF 3'S

Instead, I decided to work in 3's, and more specifically: 3 weeks, 3 months, and 3 years. It's a simple formula that not only helps you create a profitable year, but also encourages your career in the most authentic direction imaginable. Here's the process:

**#1 List what you'd like to accomplish with the rest of the year you're in.** For example, let's say you want to finish the year strong by launching a new product and doubling last year's income.

**Next ask:** If I stayed on this course, where would it get me in 3 years? Make a projection of growth and income to ensure you like where this plan leads. Per our example, you'd continue to repeat that promotion this time every year as your list grew in size.

**#2 What will I have to do in the next 3 months to get started on this plan?** This question gives birth to a progress log of tasks and to-do's. Progress logs will help you stay on track with your annual objectives, and they appear quarterly in this section.

**#3 What will I have to do in the next 3 weeks to make progress?** From there, and as my husband always chants, *nothing to it but to do it!*

---

## WHAT DO YOU WANT TO CHANGE THIS YEAR?

---

Before you set annual objectives, consider the five pillars of a harmonic life, as taught in *Harmonic Wealth: The Secret of Attracting the Life You Want* by James Arthur Ray: (1.) Financial, (2.) Spiritual, (3.) Mental, (4.) Relational, and (5.) Physical.

FINANCIAL:

SPIRITUAL:

MENTAL:

PHYSICAL:

RELATIONAL:

## annual objectives

*fill in the goals that will make 2017 feel like an absolute success*

—— EXAMPLE —— *annual objectives* —— WORKSHEET ——

**FINANCIAL:** Move our current financial situation to a better location, pay car loans, build personal and business savings, create more financial assets.

**SPIRITUAL:** Settle the mind, return to spirit. After a whirlwind of a year, I want to become more centered in the present moment, less reactionary, and more connected overall.

**MENTAL:** Catch up. Finish outstanding projects, complete outstanding studies, and build a collection of good fiction books to read as a way to recharge.

**PHYSICAL:** Quit moving this to the back-burner when times get tough; you need it more then than ever. Do workouts, meal planning, meal prep, and grocery shopping like clockwork.

**RELATIONAL:** Quality time was a much-needed escape from the frenzy this year. Leave more time for project completion, schedule more days away, eliminate the chaotic pace.

| | | |
|---|---|---|
| PAY CAR LOANS, BUILD SAVINGS | EARN $159,000 | MEDITATION & YOGA 2 X WEEK |
| WORKOUT 3 X WEEK | FINISH & IMPLEMENT ALL STUDIES | BI-MONTHLY GETAWAYS WITH FAMILY |

*quarterly progress log*

WHAT SPECIAL OCCASIONS OR EVENTS WILL YOU HONOR IN THE NEXT 3 MONTHS?

WHAT PERSONAL GOALS DO YOU NEED TO COMPLETE (OR MAKE PROGRESS) IN THE NEXT 3 MONTHS TO STAY ON TRACK WITH YOUR ANNUAL OBJECTIVES?

WHAT PROFESSIONAL GOALS DO YOU NEED TO COMPLETE (OR MAKE PROGRESS) IN THE NEXT 3 MONTHS TO STAY ON TRACK WITH YOUR ANNUAL OBJECTIVES?

*quarterly goals*

———————————————————— FINISH ————————————————————

———————————————————— DO ————————————————————

———————————————————— CELEBRATE ————————————————————

———————————————————— STUDY ————————————————————

———————————————————— START ————————————————————

*(example worksheets next page)*

## —— EXAMPLE — *quarterly progress log* — WORKSHEET ——

### WHAT SPECIAL OCCASIONS OR EVENTS WILL YOU HONOR IN THE NEXT 3 MONTHS?

- Moving house
- Your Best Year launch
- Disney vacation
- Jay's birthday
- Thanksgiving
- Christmas

### WHAT PERSONAL GOALS DO YOU NEED TO COMPLETE (OR MAKE PROGRESS) IN THE NEXT 3 MONTHS TO STAY ON TRACK WITH YOUR ANNUAL OBJECTIVES?

- Workout routine back in place
- 10,000 steps daily goal
- Come back to present: eliminate the low-grade panic
- Make new friends & connections at conference
- Enjoy family on vacation
- Enforce and honor holiday downtime

### WHAT PROFESSIONAL GOALS DO YOU NEED TO COMPLETE (OR MAKE PROGRESS) IN THE NEXT 3 MONTHS TO STAY ON TRACK WITH YOUR ANNUAL OBJECTIVES?

- Your Best Year blog posts, videos, and promotions
- Make new friends & connections at conference
- Luminaries updates
- Draft new course– have ready for production
- Outsource more to Jennie
- New Year, New You annual review

- EXAMPLE -  *quarterly goals*  - WORKSHEET -

## FINISH

* Your Best Year blogs and promos
* Moving house

## DO

* Go to conference
* Schedule holiday downtime
* Luminaries updates
* Outsource to Jennie
* New Year, New You annual review

## CELEBRATE

* new home
* family vacation
* Jay
* Thanksgiving and Christmas
* Review week

## STUDY

meditation and yoga

## START

draft new course – have it ready for production

# YOUR BEST YEAR SYSTEM

Now that you've created an annual calendar, filled in *Your Best Year* plan, and defined your annual objectives, it's time to look at the system that will help you produce it all.

For every month of 2017, you will be prompted to …

* Prioritize monthly goals (aligned with your annual objectives)
* Organize weekly task lists
* Schedule administrative days
* Record business income daily
* Assess professional strengths and weaknesses
* Identify ways to improve work - life balance

For every quarter of 2017, you will be prompted to …

* Create a progress log
* Set 3-month goals (aligned with your annual objectives)
* Update your annual strategy
* Review your progress

During every review session, identify your weak spots and time leaks, capitalize on your strengths, question your current schedule and prioritize upcoming workflow.

I encourage you to schedule at least two administrative days each month. Somebody has to clean up the mess around you, pay the bills, organize the clutter and answer your emails! Until you can afford a full-time assistant, it's going to have to be you.

Schedule your admin day at least one week into the future so you can create a running to-do list of unfinished business and knock it all out at once. Have clear goals for the day, such as, an empty inbox, a tidy office, a list of inventory and a revised budget.

In online business, it's important to respect all of the different hats you wear. Your CEO hat (planning, review, decision-making) is as important as your secretary hat (admin, organization and scheduling) and vice versa. In order to run an efficient operation, take time for these things every month.

# TRACK YOUR ABUNDANCE

A new addition to the system this year is a worksheet for daily abundance tracking. If you're anything like I was, you check your email all day, literally *waiting* for sales to come in. Because I checked and deleted all day, I really had no idea how much I earned.

This happened last October when *Your Best Year 2016* first launched. I had four pages of sales, all bold and unread, and I carried my laptop over to each family member and made them sit there while I arrowed through the pages!

When it was over, all that was left for me to do was delete all the sales notifications to clear my inbox. And before I knew it, I was back to checking hourly for more sales.

Then I read the book, *Get Rich, Lucky Bitch!* by Denise Duffield-Thomas and everything changed. Her idea to track and record abundance was one of my favorite takeaways, and I've adapted this into a worksheet for your monthly review.

Here's the gist: Money flows into your life every day, and unless you record it, you really have no idea how wealthy you are or how healthy your business is. Each month, I write a financial goal that challenges me, then think of a reward for achieving it.

I have shattered income ceilings using this method in 2016, rewarding myself things, such as a bi-weekly housecleaning crew, a Disney Cruse for my family, a private sitting room sanctuary for myself, and a spontaneous trip to San Francisco – all paid in full.

I visit my abundance tracker every morning and record the previous day's income before deleting payment notifications and completed orders. At the top of the worksheet, I write a few things I'm trying to accomplish that month (i.e. "Offset a project-building month, attract interested clients").

Down below, I list some ways to achieve my goal (i.e. "course launch, book clearance, membership dues"). I also use that space below to list financial goals I'll complete by meeting this income (i.e. "Car paid, savings goal met, one-month salary in reserve").

I hope this exercise becomes as profitable for you as it's been for me. You'll find it on the third page of each monthly review.

## *January focus*

**FINANCIAL:**

**SPIRITUAL:**

**MENTAL:**

**PHYSICAL:**

**RELATIONAL:**

## *tasks to complete*

| WEEK OF THE 2ND | WEEK OF THE 9TH | WEEK OF THE 16TH | WEEK OF THE 23RD | WEEK OF THE 30TH |
|---|---|---|---|---|
| | | | | |

*don't forget to add admin days to the list!*

*January abundance*

## MONTHLY CHALLENGE:

### TO ACCOMPLISH THIS MONTH:

EARN _____ IN JANUARY!

| 01/01 | WEEK 1 | 01/14 | 01/20 | 01/26 |
| 01/02 | 01/08 | WEEK 2 | 01/21 | 01/27 |
| 01/03 | 01/09 | 01/15 | WEEK 3 | 01/28 |
| 01/04 | 01/10 | 01/16 | 01/22 | WEEK 4 |
| 01/05 | 01/11 | 01/17 | 01/23 | 01/29 |
| 01/06 | 01/12 | 01/18 | 01/24 | 01/30 |
| 01/07 | 01/13 | 01/19 | 01/25 | 01/31 |

TOTAL EARNED:

IDEAS TO HELP MEET THIS CHALLENGE:

## REWARD:

## *January review*

GROWTH TRACKER - RECORD YOUR END-MONTH NUMBERS, FANS, AND FOLLOWERS.

FB    PINTEREST    EMAIL    VIEWS    SALES    [        ]    [        ]    [        ]    [        ]

_____    _____    _____    _____    _____    _____    _____    _____

*circle the metrics you will work to improve next month*

GOAL TRACKER - RECORD YOUR PROGRESS AND CHALLENGES THIS MONTH.

FINANCIAL:

SPIRITUAL:

MENTAL:

PHYSICAL:

RELATIONAL:

MOST IMPORTANT TO ME RIGHT NOW?
_____

DOES MY SCHEDULE NEED REARRANGED?
_____

PROFIT TRACKER - RECORD THIS MONTH'S INCOME, SALARY, AND EXPENSES.

TOTAL EARNED (YEAR-TO-DATE):

## *January review*

### PROJECTS COMPLETED THIS MONTH

### WHAT WORKED WELL THIS MONTH?

### AND WHY?

HOW CAN I MULTIPLY THESE RESULTS?

### PROJECTS STILL IN THE WORKS

### DID THIS MONTH GET ME CLOSER TO MY ANNUAL OBJECTIVES?

IF YES, HOW WILL I KEEP UP THE MOMENTUM?

IF NO, WHAT WILL I DO TO GET BACK ON TRACK?

### WHAT OBSTACLE(S) AM I FACING?

WHY IS IT DIFFICULT?

HOW HAVE I TRIED TO OVERCOME IT?

WHAT CAN I TRY NEXT?

## February focus

**FINANCIAL:**

**SPIRITUAL:**

**MENTAL:**

**PHYSICAL:**

**RELATIONAL:**

## tasks to complete

| WEEK OF THE 30TH | WEEK OF THE 6TH | WEEK OF THE 13TH | WEEK OF THE 20TH | WEEK OF THE 27TH |
|---|---|---|---|---|
| | | | | |

*don't forget to add admin days to the list!*

*February abundance*

# MONTHLY CHALLENGE:

TO ACCOMPLISH THIS MONTH:

EARN _____ IN FEBRUARY!

| 02/01 | WEEK 1 | 02/14 | 02/20 | 02/26 |
| 02/02 | 02/08 | WEEK 2 | 02/21 | 02/27 |
| 02/03 | 02/09 | 02/15 | WEEK 3 | 02/28 |
| 02/04 | 02/10 | 02/16 | 02/22 | WEEK 4 |
| 02/05 | 02/11 | 02/17 | 02/23 | |
| 02/06 | 02/12 | 02/18 | 02/24 | |
| 02/07 | 02/13 | 02/19 | 02/25 | |

TOTAL EARNED:

# REWARD:

IDEAS TO HELP MEET THIS CHALLENGE:

*February review*

GROWTH TRACKER - RECORD YOUR END-MONTH NUMBERS, FANS, AND FOLLOWERS.

FB     PINTEREST     EMAIL     VIEWS     SALES     [          ]   [          ]   [          ]   [          ]

_____   _____   _____   _____   _____   _____   _____   _____

*circle the metrics you will work to improve next month*

GOAL TRACKER - RECORD YOUR PROGRESS AND CHALLENGES THIS MONTH.

FINANCIAL:

SPIRITUAL:

MENTAL:

PHYSICAL:

RELATIONAL:

MOST IMPORTANT TO ME RIGHT NOW?
_____

DOES MY SCHEDULE NEED REARRANGED?
_____

PROFIT TRACKER - RECORD THIS MONTH'S INCOME, SALARY, AND EXPENSES.

TOTAL EARNED (YEAR-TO-DATE):

## February review

### PROJECTS COMPLETED THIS MONTH

### WHAT WORKED WELL THIS MONTH?

AND WHY?

HOW CAN I MULTIPLY THESE RESULTS?

### PROJECTS STILL IN THE WORKS

### DID THIS MONTH GET ME CLOSER TO MY ANNUAL OBJECTIVES?

IF YES, HOW WILL I KEEP UP THE MOMENTUM?

IF NO, WHAT WILL I DO TO GET BACK ON TRACK?

### WHAT OBSTACLE(S) AM I FACING?

WHY IS IT DIFFICULT?

HOW HAVE I TRIED TO OVERCOME IT?

WHAT CAN I TRY NEXT?

## March focus

**FINANCIAL:**

**SPIRITUAL:**

**MENTAL:**

**PHYSICAL:**

**RELATIONAL:**

## tasks to complete

| WEEK OF THE 27TH | WEEK OF THE 6TH | WEEK OF THE 13TH | WEEK OF THE 20TH | WEEK OF THE 27TH |
|---|---|---|---|---|
| | | | | |

*don't forget to add admin days to the list!*

## March abundance

## MONTHLY CHALLENGE:

TO ACCOMPLISH THIS MONTH:

EARN _____ IN MARCH!

| 03/01 | WEEK 1 | 03/14 | 03/20 | 03/26 |
| 03/02 | 03/08 | WEEK 2 | 03/21 | 03/27 |
| 03/03 | 03/09 | 03/15 | WEEK 3 | 03/28 |
| 03/04 | 03/10 | 03/16 | 03/22 | WEEK 4 |
| 03/05 | 03/11 | 03/17 | 03/23 | 03/29 |
| 03/06 | 03/12 | 03/18 | 03/24 | 03/30 |
| 03/07 | 03/13 | 03/19 | 03/25 | 03/31 |

TOTAL EARNED:

IDEAS TO HELP MEET THIS CHALLENGE:

## REWARD:

## *March review*

GROWTH TRACKER - RECORD YOUR END-MONTH NUMBERS, FANS, AND FOLLOWERS.

FB    PINTEREST    EMAIL    VIEWS    SALES    [        ]  [        ]  [        ]  [        ]

_____    _____    _____    _____    _____    _____    _____    _____    _____

*circle the metrics you will work to improve next month*

GOAL TRACKER - RECORD YOUR PROGRESS AND CHALLENGES THIS MONTH.

FINANCIAL:

SPIRITUAL:

MENTAL:

PHYSICAL:

RELATIONAL:

MOST IMPORTANT TO ME RIGHT NOW?
_____

DOES MY SCHEDULE NEED REARRANGED?
_____

PROFIT TRACKER - RECORD THIS MONTH'S INCOME, SALARY, AND EXPENSES.

TOTAL EARNED (YEAR-TO-DATE):

## March review

### PROJECTS COMPLETED THIS MONTH

### WHAT WORKED WELL THIS MONTH?

### AND WHY?

HOW CAN I MULTIPLY THESE RESULTS?

### PROJECTS STILL IN THE WORKS

### DID THIS MONTH GET ME CLOSER TO MY ANNUAL OBJECTIVES?

IF YES, HOW WILL I KEEP UP THE MOMENTUM?

IF NO, WHAT WILL I DO TO GET BACK ON TRACK?

### WHAT OBSTACLE(S) AM I FACING?

WHY IS IT DIFFICULT?

HOW HAVE I TRIED TO OVERCOME IT?

WHAT CAN I TRY NEXT?

*quarterly progress log*

WHAT SPECIAL OCCASIONS OR EVENTS WILL YOU HONOR IN THE NEXT 3 MONTHS?

WHAT PERSONAL GOALS DO YOU NEED TO COMPLETE (OR MAKE PROGRESS) IN THE NEXT 3 MONTHS TO STAY ON TRACK WITH YOUR ANNUAL OBJECTIVES?

WHAT PROFESSIONAL GOALS DO YOU NEED TO COMPLETE (OR MAKE PROGRESS) IN THE NEXT 3 MONTHS TO STAY ON TRACK WITH YOUR ANNUAL OBJECTIVES?

## quarterly goals

———————————————————— FINISH ————————————————————

———————————————————— DO ————————————————————

———————————————————— CELEBRATE ————————————————————

———————————————————— STUDY ————————————————————

———————————————————— START ————————————————————

# YOUR ANNUAL STRATEGY

| APRIL | MAY | JUNE | JULY |
|---|---|---|---|

| AUGUST | SEPTEMBER | OCTOBER | NOVEMBER |
|---|---|---|---|

| DECEMBER | JANUARY | FEBRUARY | MARCH |
|---|---|---|---|

─────────── *quarterly review* ───────────

WHAT ARE YOUR FAVORITE MEMORIES?          WHAT WAS TIME VERY WELL SPENT?

─────────────────────────                 ─────────────────────────

WHAT DID YOU ACCOMPLISH OR COMPLETE?       WHAT WAS MONEY VERY WELL SPENT?

HAVE YOU MADE PROGRESS ON YOUR ANNUAL OBJECTIVES?

WHAT ARE YOUR OUTSTANDING GOALS?           WHAT WAS YOUR WORST SETBACK?

ARE YOU KEEPING ANY BAD HABITS?            WHAT'S HOLDING YOU BACK?

## *April focus*

**FINANCIAL:**

**SPIRITUAL:**

**MENTAL:**

**PHYSICAL:**

**RELATIONAL:**

## *tasks to complete*

| WEEK OF THE 27TH | WEEK OF THE 3RD | WEEK OF THE 10TH | WEEK OF THE 17TH | WEEK OF THE 24TH |
|---|---|---|---|---|
| | | | | |

*don't forget to add admin days to the list!*

## April abundance

# MONTHLY CHALLENGE:

EARN _____ IN APRIL!

TO ACCOMPLISH THIS MONTH:

| 04/01 | WEEK 1 | 04/14 | 04/20 | 04/26 |
| 04/02 | 04/08 | WEEK 2 | 04/21 | 04/27 |
| 04/03 | 04/09 | 04/15 | WEEK 3 | 04/28 |
| 04/04 | 04/10 | 04/16 | 04/22 | WEEK 4 |
| 04/05 | 04/11 | 04/17 | 04/23 | 04/29 |
| 04/06 | 04/12 | 04/18 | 04/24 | 04/30 |
| 04/07 | 04/13 | 04/19 | 04/25 | |

TOTAL EARNED:

IDEAS TO HELP MEET THIS CHALLENGE:

# REWARD:

## *April review*

GROWTH TRACKER - RECORD YOUR END-MONTH NUMBERS, FANS, AND FOLLOWERS.

FB    PINTEREST    EMAIL    VIEWS    SALES    [        ]  [        ]  [        ]  [        ]

_____    _____    _____    _____    _____    _____    _____    _____    _____

*circle the metrics you will work to improve next month*

GOAL TRACKER - RECORD YOUR PROGRESS AND CHALLENGES THIS MONTH.

FINANCIAL:

SPIRITUAL:

MENTAL:

PHYSICAL:

RELATIONAL:

MOST IMPORTANT TO ME
RIGHT NOW?
_____

DOES MY SCHEDULE
NEED REARRANGED?
_____

PROFIT TRACKER - RECORD THIS MONTH'S INCOME, SALARY, AND EXPENSES.

TOTAL EARNED (YEAR-TO-DATE):

## April review

### PROJECTS COMPLETED THIS MONTH

### WHAT WORKED WELL THIS MONTH?

### AND WHY?

HOW CAN I MULTIPLY THESE RESULTS?

### PROJECTS STILL IN THE WORKS

### DID THIS MONTH GET ME CLOSER TO MY ANNUAL OBJECTIVES?

IF YES, HOW WILL I KEEP UP THE MOMENTUM?

IF NO, WHAT WILL I DO TO GET BACK ON TRACK?

### WHAT OBSTACLE(S) AM I FACING?

WHY IS IT DIFFICULT?

HOW HAVE I TRIED TO OVERCOME IT?

WHAT CAN I TRY NEXT?

## *May focus*

**FINANCIAL:**

**SPIRITUAL:**

**MENTAL:**

**PHYSICAL:**

**RELATIONAL:**

## *tasks to complete*

| WEEK OF THE 1ST | WEEK OF THE 8TH | WEEK OF THE 15TH | WEEK OF THE 22ND | WEEK OF THE 29TH |
|---|---|---|---|---|
| | | | | |

*don't forget to add admin days to the list!*

*May abundance*

## MONTHLY CHALLENGE:

TO ACCOMPLISH THIS MONTH:

EARN                    IN MAY!

| | | | | |
|---|---|---|---|---|
| 05/01 | ✦ WEEK 1 ✦ | 05/14 | 05/20 | 05/26 |
| 05/02 | 05/08 | ✦ WEEK 2 ✦ | 05/21 | 05/27 |
| 05/03 | 05/09 | 05/15 | ✦ WEEK 3 ✦ | 05/28 |
| 05/04 | 05/10 | 05/16 | 05/22 | ✦ WEEK 4 ✦ |
| 05/05 | 05/11 | 05/17 | 05/23 | 05/29 |
| 05/06 | 05/12 | 05/18 | 05/24 | 05/30 |
| 05/07 | 05/13 | 05/19 | 05/25 | 05/31 |

✦ TOTAL EARNED:

IDEAS TO HELP MEET THIS CHALLENGE:

## REWARD:

*May review*

GROWTH TRACKER - RECORD YOUR END-MONTH NUMBERS, FANS, AND FOLLOWERS.

FB    PINTEREST    EMAIL    VIEWS    SALES    [        ]  [        ]  [        ]  [        ]

———    ———    ———    ———    ———    ———    ———    ———    ———

*circle the metrics you will work to improve next month*

GOAL TRACKER - RECORD YOUR PROGRESS AND CHALLENGES THIS MONTH.

FINANCIAL:

SPIRITUAL:

MENTAL:

PHYSICAL:

RELATIONAL:

MOST IMPORTANT TO ME
RIGHT NOW?
_____

DOES MY SCHEDULE
NEED REARRANGED?
_____

PROFIT TRACKER - RECORD THIS MONTH'S INCOME, SALARY, AND EXPENSES.

TOTAL EARNED (YEAR-TO-DATE):

## May review

### PROJECTS COMPLETED THIS MONTH

### WHAT WORKED WELL THIS MONTH?

### AND WHY?

HOW CAN I MULTIPLY THESE RESULTS?

### PROJECTS STILL IN THE WORKS

### DID THIS MONTH GET ME CLOSER TO MY ANNUAL OBJECTIVES?

IF YES, HOW WILL I KEEP UP THE MOMENTUM?

IF NO, WHAT WILL I DO TO GET BACK ON TRACK?

### WHAT OBSTACLE(S) AM I FACING?

WHY IS IT DIFFICULT?

HOW HAVE I TRIED TO OVERCOME IT?

WHAT CAN I TRY NEXT?

## *June focus*

**FINANCIAL:**

**SPIRITUAL:**

**MENTAL:**

**PHYSICAL:**

**RELATIONAL:**

## *tasks to complete*

| WEEK OF THE 29TH | WEEK OF THE 5TH | WEEK OF THE 12TH | WEEK OF THE 19TH | WEEK OF THE 26TH |
|---|---|---|---|---|
|  |  |  |  |  |

*don't forget to add admin days to the list!*

*June abundance*

# MONTHLY CHALLENGE:

## TO ACCOMPLISH THIS MONTH:

EARN _____ IN JUNE!

| 06/01 | ⭐ WEEK 1 ⭐ | 06/14 | 06/20 | 06/26 |

| 06/02 | 06/08 | ⭐ WEEK 2 ⭐ | 06/21 | 06/27 |

| 06/03 | 06/09 | 06/15 | ⭐ WEEK 3 ⭐ | 06/28 |

| 06/04 | 06/10 | 06/16 | 06/22 | ⭐ WEEK 4 ⭐ |

| 06/05 | 06/11 | 06/17 | 06/23 | 06/29 |

| 06/06 | 06/12 | 06/18 | 06/24 | 06/30 |

| 06/07 | 06/13 | 06/19 | 06/25 | |

⭐ TOTAL EARNED:

IDEAS TO HELP MEET THIS CHALLENGE:

# REWARD:

*June review*

## GROWTH TRACKER — RECORD YOUR END-MONTH NUMBERS, FANS, AND FOLLOWERS.

FB    PINTEREST    EMAIL    VIEWS    SALES   [     ]  [     ]  [     ]  [     ]

_____   _____   _____   _____   _____   _____   _____   _____

*circle the metrics you will work to improve next month*

## GOAL TRACKER — RECORD YOUR PROGRESS AND CHALLENGES THIS MONTH.

FINANCIAL:

SPIRITUAL:

MENTAL:

PHYSICAL:

RELATIONAL:

> **MOST IMPORTANT TO ME RIGHT NOW?**
> _____

> **DOES MY SCHEDULE NEED REARRANGED?**
> _____

## PROFIT TRACKER — RECORD THIS MONTH'S INCOME, SALARY, AND EXPENSES.

TOTAL EARNED (YEAR-TO-DATE):

## June review

### PROJECTS COMPLETED THIS MONTH

### WHAT WORKED WELL THIS MONTH?

### AND WHY?

HOW CAN I MULTIPLY THESE RESULTS?

### PROJECTS STILL IN THE WORKS

### DID THIS MONTH GET ME CLOSER TO MY ANNUAL OBJECTIVES?

IF YES, HOW WILL I KEEP UP THE MOMENTUM?

IF NO, WHAT WILL I DO TO GET BACK ON TRACK?

### WHAT OBSTACLE(S) AM I FACING?

WHY IS IT DIFFICULT?

HOW HAVE I TRIED TO OVERCOME IT?

WHAT CAN I TRY NEXT?

——————————— *quarterly progress log* ———————————

WHAT SPECIAL OCCASIONS OR EVENTS WILL YOU HONOR IN THE NEXT 3 MONTHS?

WHAT PERSONAL GOALS DO YOU NEED TO COMPLETE (OR MAKE PROGRESS) IN THE NEXT 3 MONTHS TO STAY ON TRACK WITH YOUR ANNUAL OBJECTIVES?

WHAT PROFESSIONAL GOALS DO YOU NEED TO COMPLETE (OR MAKE PROGRESS) IN THE NEXT 3 MONTHS TO STAY ON TRACK WITH YOUR ANNUAL OBJECTIVES?

## *quarterly goals*

———— FINISH ————

———— DO ————

———— CELEBRATE ————

———— STUDY ————

———— START ————

# YOUR ANNUAL STRATEGY

| JULY | AUGUST | SEPTEMBER | OCTOBER |
|------|--------|-----------|---------|

| NOVEMBER | DECEMBER | JANUARY | FEBRUARY |
|----------|----------|---------|----------|

| MARCH | APRIL | MAY | JUNE |
|-------|-------|-----|------|

—— *quarterly review* ——

WHAT ARE YOUR FAVORITE MEMORIES?　　　⏰ WHAT WAS TIME VERY WELL SPENT?

WHAT DID YOU ACCOMPLISH OR COMPLETE?　　💰 WHAT WAS MONEY VERY WELL SPENT?

HAVE YOU MADE PROGRESS ON YOUR ANNUAL OBJECTIVES?

WHAT ARE YOUR OUTSTANDING GOALS?　　　　WHAT WAS YOUR WORST SETBACK?

ARE YOU KEEPING ANY BAD HABITS?　　　　⚙ WHAT'S HOLDING YOU BACK?

## July focus

**FINANCIAL:**

**SPIRITUAL:**

**MENTAL:**

**PHYSICAL:**

**RELATIONAL:**

## tasks to complete

| WEEK OF THE 3RD | WEEK OF THE 10TH | WEEK OF THE 17TH | WEEK OF THE 24TH | WEEK OF THE 31ST |
| --- | --- | --- | --- | --- |
| | | | | |

*don't forget to add admin days to the list!*

*July abundance*

## MONTHLY CHALLENGE:

TO ACCOMPLISH THIS MONTH:

EARN                    IN JULY!

| 07/01 | WEEK 1 | 07/14 | 07/20 | 07/26 |
| 07/02 | 07/08 | WEEK 2 | 07/21 | 07/27 |
| 07/03 | 07/09 | 07/15 | WEEK 3 | 07/28 |
| 07/04 | 07/10 | 07/16 | 07/22 | WEEK 4 |
| 07/05 | 07/11 | 07/17 | 07/23 | 07/29 |
| 07/06 | 07/12 | 07/18 | 07/24 | 07/30 |
| 07/07 | 07/13 | 07/19 | 07/25 | 07/31 |

TOTAL EARNED:

IDEAS TO HELP MEET THIS CHALLENGE:

## REWARD:

*July review*

GROWTH TRACKER - RECORD YOUR END-MONTH NUMBERS, FANS, AND FOLLOWERS.

FB    PINTEREST    EMAIL    VIEWS    SALES    [        ]  [        ]  [        ]  [        ]

____    ____    ____    ____    ____    ____    ____    ____    ____

*circle the metrics you will work to improve next month*

GOAL TRACKER - RECORD YOUR PROGRESS AND CHALLENGES THIS MONTH.

FINANCIAL:

SPIRITUAL:

MENTAL:

PHYSICAL:

RELATIONAL:

MOST IMPORTANT TO ME RIGHT NOW?
_____

DOES MY SCHEDULE NEED REARRANGED?
_____

PROFIT TRACKER - RECORD THIS MONTH'S INCOME, SALARY, AND EXPENSES.

TOTAL EARNED (YEAR-TO-DATE):

## *July review*

### PROJECTS COMPLETED THIS MONTH

### WHAT WORKED WELL THIS MONTH?

AND WHY?

HOW CAN I MULTIPLY THESE RESULTS?

### PROJECTS STILL IN THE WORKS

### DID THIS MONTH GET ME CLOSER
### TO MY ANNUAL OBJECTIVES?

IF YES, HOW WILL I KEEP UP THE MOMENTUM?

IF NO, WHAT WILL I DO TO GET BACK ON TRACK?

### WHAT OBSTACLE(S) AM I FACING?

WHY IS IT DIFFICULT?

HOW HAVE I TRIED TO OVERCOME IT?

WHAT CAN I TRY NEXT?

## *August focus*

**FINANCIAL:**

**SPIRITUAL:**

**MENTAL:**

**PHYSICAL:**

**RELATIONAL:**

## *tasks to complete*

| WEEK OF THE 31ST | WEEK OF THE 7TH | WEEK OF THE 14TH | WEEK OF THE 21ST | WEEK OF THE 28TH |
|---|---|---|---|---|
| | | | | |

*don't forget to add admin days to the list!*

*August abundance*

# MONTHLY CHALLENGE:

TO ACCOMPLISH THIS MONTH:

EARN _____ IN AUGUST!

| 08/01 | WEEK 1 | 08/14 | 08/20 | 08/26 |
| 08/02 | 08/08 | WEEK 2 | 08/21 | 08/27 |
| 08/03 | 08/09 | 08/15 | WEEK 3 | 08/28 |
| 08/04 | 08/10 | 08/16 | 08/22 | WEEK 4 |
| 08/05 | 08/11 | 08/17 | 08/23 | 08/29 |
| 08/06 | 08/12 | 08/18 | 08/24 | 08/30 |
| 08/07 | 08/13 | 08/19 | 08/25 | 08/31 |

TOTAL EARNED:

IDEAS TO HELP MEET THIS CHALLENGE:

# REWARD:

## *August review*

GROWTH TRACKER – RECORD YOUR END-MONTH NUMBERS, FANS, AND FOLLOWERS.

FB     PINTEREST    EMAIL     VIEWS     SALES     [          ]  [          ]  [          ]  [          ]

_____     _____     _____     _____     _____     _____     _____     _____     _____

*circle the metrics you will work to improve next month*

GOAL TRACKER – RECORD YOUR PROGRESS AND CHALLENGES THIS MONTH.

FINANCIAL:

SPIRITUAL:

MENTAL:

PHYSICAL:

RELATIONAL:

MOST IMPORTANT TO ME RIGHT NOW?
_____

DOES MY SCHEDULE NEED REARRANGED?
_____

PROFIT TRACKER – RECORD THIS MONTH'S INCOME, SALARY, AND EXPENSES.

TOTAL EARNED (YEAR-TO-DATE):

## *August review*

### PROJECTS COMPLETED THIS MONTH

### WHAT WORKED WELL THIS MONTH?

### AND WHY?

HOW CAN I MULTIPLY THESE RESULTS?

### PROJECTS STILL IN THE WORKS

### DID THIS MONTH GET ME CLOSER TO MY ANNUAL OBJECTIVES?

IF YES, HOW WILL I KEEP UP THE MOMENTUM?

IF NO, WHAT WILL I DO TO GET BACK ON TRACK?

### WHAT OBSTACLE(S) AM I FACING?

WHY IS IT DIFFICULT?

HOW HAVE I TRIED TO OVERCOME IT?

WHAT CAN I TRY NEXT?

## September focus

FINANCIAL:

SPIRITUAL:

MENTAL:

PHYSICAL:

RELATIONAL:

## tasks to complete

| WEEK OF THE 28TH | WEEK OF THE 4TH | WEEK OF THE 11TH | WEEK OF THE 18TH | WEEK OF THE 25TH |
|---|---|---|---|---|
| | | | | |

*don't forget to add admin days to the list!*

*September abundance*

# MONTHLY CHALLENGE:

TO ACCOMPLISH THIS MONTH:

EARN                    IN SEPTEMBER!

| 09/01 | WEEK 1 | 09/14 | 09/20 | 09/26 |

| 09/02 | 09/08 | WEEK 2 | 09/21 | 09/27 |

| 09/03 | 09/09 | 09/15 | WEEK 3 | 09/28 |

| 09/04 | 09/10 | 09/16 | 09/22 | WEEK 4 |

| 09/05 | 09/11 | 09/17 | 09/23 | 09/29 |

| 09/06 | 09/12 | 09/18 | 09/24 | 09/30 |

| 09/07 | 09/13 | 09/19 | 09/25 | |

TOTAL EARNED:

# REWARD:

IDEAS TO HELP MEET THIS CHALLENGE:

*September review*

GROWTH TRACKER – RECORD YOUR END-MONTH NUMBERS, FANS, AND FOLLOWERS.

FB    PINTEREST    EMAIL    VIEWS    SALES    [          ]  [          ]  [          ]  [          ]

_____    _____    _____    _____    _____    _____    _____    _____

*circle the metrics you will work to improve next month*

GOAL TRACKER – RECORD YOUR PROGRESS AND CHALLENGES THIS MONTH.

FINANCIAL:

SPIRITUAL:

MENTAL:

PHYSICAL:

RELATIONAL:

```
┌─────────────────────────┐
│   MOST IMPORTANT TO ME   │
│       RIGHT NOW?         │
│   _____    │
│                          │
│                          │
└─────────────────────────┘

┌─────────────────────────┐
│    DOES MY SCHEDULE      │
│    NEED REARRANGED?      │
│   _____    │
│                          │
│                          │
└─────────────────────────┘
```

PROFIT TRACKER – RECORD THIS MONTH'S INCOME, SALARY, AND EXPENSES.

TOTAL EARNED (YEAR-TO-DATE):

## September review

### PROJECTS COMPLETED THIS MONTH

### WHAT WORKED WELL THIS MONTH?

AND WHY?

HOW CAN I MULTIPLY THESE RESULTS?

### PROJECTS STILL IN THE WORKS

### DID THIS MONTH GET ME CLOSER TO MY ANNUAL OBJECTIVES?

IF YES, HOW WILL I KEEP UP THE MOMENTUM?

IF NO, WHAT WILL I DO TO GET BACK ON TRACK?

### WHAT OBSTACLE(S) AM I FACING?

WHY IS IT DIFFICULT?

HOW HAVE I TRIED TO OVERCOME IT?

WHAT CAN I TRY NEXT?

*———— quarterly progress log ————*

WHAT SPECIAL OCCASIONS OR EVENTS WILL YOU HONOR IN THE NEXT 3 MONTHS?

WHAT PERSONAL GOALS DO YOU NEED TO COMPLETE (OR MAKE PROGRESS) IN THE NEXT 3 MONTHS TO STAY ON TRACK WITH YOUR ANNUAL OBJECTIVES?

WHAT PROFESSIONAL GOALS DO YOU NEED TO COMPLETE (OR MAKE PROGRESS) IN THE NEXT 3 MONTHS TO STAY ON TRACK WITH YOUR ANNUAL OBJECTIVES?

# *quarterly goals*

———————————————————— FINISH ————————————————————

———————————————————— DO ————————————————————

———————————————————— CELEBRATE ————————————————————

———————————————————— STUDY ————————————————————

———————————————————— START ————————————————————

# YOUR ANNUAL STRATEGY

| OCTOBER | NOVEMBER | DECEMBER | JANUARY |
| --- | --- | --- | --- |

| FEBRUARY | MARCH | APRIL | MAY |
| --- | --- | --- | --- |

| JUNE | JULY | AUGUST | SEPTEMBER |
| --- | --- | --- | --- |

*quarterly review*

WHAT ARE YOUR FAVORITE MEMORIES?

WHAT WAS TIME VERY WELL SPENT?

WHAT DID YOU ACCOMPLISH OR COMPLETE?

WHAT WAS MONEY VERY WELL SPENT?

HAVE YOU MADE PROGRESS ON YOUR ANNUAL OBJECTIVES?

WHAT ARE YOUR OUTSTANDING GOALS?

WHAT WAS YOUR WORST SETBACK?

ARE YOU KEEPING ANY BAD HABITS?

WHAT'S HOLDING YOU BACK?

## October focus

FINANCIAL:

SPIRITUAL:

MENTAL:

PHYSICAL:

RELATIONAL:

## tasks to complete

| WEEK OF THE 2ND | WEEK OF THE 9TH | WEEK OF THE 16TH | WEEK OF THE 23RD | WEEK OF THE 30TH |
|---|---|---|---|---|
| | | | | |

*don't forget to add admin days to the list!*

## October abundance

# MONTHLY CHALLENGE:

TO ACCOMPLISH THIS MONTH:

EARN        IN OCTOBER!

| | | | | |
|---|---|---|---|---|
| 10/01 | WEEK 1 | 10/14 | 10/20 | 10/26 |
| 10/02 | 10/08 | WEEK 2 | 10/21 | 10/27 |
| 10/03 | 10/09 | 10/15 | WEEK 3 | 10/28 |
| 10/04 | 10/10 | 10/16 | 10/22 | WEEK 4 |
| 10/05 | 10/11 | 10/17 | 10/23 | 10/29 |
| 10/06 | 10/12 | 10/18 | 10/24 | 10/30 |
| 10/07 | 10/13 | 10/19 | 10/25 | 10/31 |

TOTAL EARNED:

IDEAS TO HELP MEET THIS CHALLENGE:

# REWARD:

## *October review*

GROWTH TRACKER - RECORD YOUR END-MONTH NUMBERS, FANS, AND FOLLOWERS.

FB    PINTEREST    EMAIL    VIEWS    SALES    [        ]    [        ]    [        ]    [        ]

_____    _____    _____    _____    _____    _____    _____    _____    _____

*circle the metrics you will work to improve next month*

GOAL TRACKER - RECORD YOUR PROGRESS AND CHALLENGES THIS MONTH.

FINANCIAL:

SPIRITUAL:

MENTAL:

PHYSICAL:

RELATIONAL:

MOST IMPORTANT TO ME RIGHT NOW?
_____

DOES MY SCHEDULE NEED REARRANGED?
_____

PROFIT TRACKER - RECORD THIS MONTH'S INCOME, SALARY, AND EXPENSES.

TOTAL EARNED (YEAR-TO-DATE):

## October review

### PROJECTS COMPLETED THIS MONTH

### WHAT WORKED WELL THIS MONTH?

AND WHY?

HOW CAN I MULTIPLY THESE RESULTS?

### PROJECTS STILL IN THE WORKS

### DID THIS MONTH GET ME CLOSER TO MY ANNUAL OBJECTIVES?

IF YES, HOW WILL I KEEP UP THE MOMENTUM?

IF NO, WHAT WILL I DO TO GET BACK ON TRACK?

### WHAT OBSTACLE(S) AM I FACING?

WHY IS IT DIFFICULT?

HOW HAVE I TRIED TO OVERCOME IT?

WHAT CAN I TRY NEXT?

## *November focus*

**FINANCIAL:**

**SPIRITUAL:**

**MENTAL:**

**PHYSICAL:**

**RELATIONAL:**

## *tasks to complete*

| WEEK OF THE 30TH | WEEK OF THE 6TH | WEEK OF THE 13TH | WEEK OF THE 20TH | WEEK OF THE 27TH |
|---|---|---|---|---|
| | | | | |

*don't forget to add admin days to the list!*

*November abundance*

## MONTHLY CHALLENGE:

TO ACCOMPLISH THIS MONTH:

EARN _____ IN NOVEMBER!

| 11/01 | WEEK 1 | 11/14 | 11/20 | 11/26 |
| 11/02 | 11/08 | WEEK 2 | 11/21 | 11/27 |
| 11/03 | 11/09 | 11/15 | WEEK 3 | 11/28 |
| 11/04 | 11/10 | 11/16 | 11/22 | WEEK 4 |
| 11/05 | 11/11 | 11/17 | 11/23 | 11/29 |
| 11/06 | 11/12 | 11/18 | 11/24 | 11/30 |
| 11/07 | 11/13 | 11/19 | 11/25 | |

TOTAL EARNED:

IDEAS TO HELP MEET THIS CHALLENGE:

## REWARD:

## *November review*

GROWTH TRACKER - RECORD YOUR END-MONTH NUMBERS, FANS, AND FOLLOWERS.

FB    PINTEREST    EMAIL    VIEWS    SALES    [        ]  [        ]  [        ]  [        ]

_____   _____   _____   _____   _____   _____   _____   _____

*circle the metrics you will work to improve next month*

GOAL TRACKER - RECORD YOUR PROGRESS AND CHALLENGES THIS MONTH.

FINANCIAL:

SPIRITUAL:

MENTAL:

PHYSICAL:

RELATIONAL:

MOST IMPORTANT TO ME RIGHT NOW?
_____

DOES MY SCHEDULE NEED REARRANGED?
_____

PROFIT TRACKER - RECORD THIS MONTH'S INCOME, SALARY, AND EXPENSES.

TOTAL EARNED (YEAR-TO-DATE):

## November review

### PROJECTS COMPLETED THIS MONTH

### WHAT WORKED WELL THIS MONTH?

### AND WHY?

HOW CAN I MULTIPLY THESE RESULTS?

### PROJECTS STILL IN THE WORKS

### DID THIS MONTH GET ME CLOSER TO MY ANNUAL OBJECTIVES?

IF YES, HOW WILL I KEEP UP THE MOMENTUM?

IF NO, WHAT WILL I DO TO GET BACK ON TRACK?

### WHAT OBSTACLE(S) AM I FACING?

WHY IS IT DIFFICULT?

HOW HAVE I TRIED TO OVERCOME IT?

WHAT CAN I TRY NEXT?

*December focus*

**FINANCIAL:**

**SPIRITUAL:**

**MENTAL:**

**PHYSICAL:**

**RELATIONAL:**

*tasks to complete*

| WEEK OF THE 27TH | WEEK OF THE 4TH | WEEK OF THE 11TH | WEEK OF THE 18TH | WEEK OF THE 25TH |
| --- | --- | --- | --- | --- |
| | | | | |

*don't forget to add admin days to the list!*

*December abundance*

## MONTHLY CHALLENGE:

TO ACCOMPLISH THIS MONTH:

EARN _____ IN DECEMBER!

| 12/01 | WEEK 1 | 12/14 | 12/20 | 12/26 |
| 12/02 | 12/08 | WEEK 2 | 12/21 | 12/27 |
| 12/03 | 12/09 | 12/15 | WEEK 3 | 12/28 |
| 12/04 | 12/10 | 12/16 | 12/22 | WEEK 4 |
| 12/05 | 12/11 | 12/17 | 12/23 | 12/29 |
| 12/06 | 12/12 | 12/18 | 12/24 | 12/30 |
| 12/07 | 12/13 | 12/19 | 12/25 | 12/31 |

TOTAL EARNED:

IDEAS TO HELP MEET THIS CHALLENGE:

## REWARD:

*December review*

GROWTH TRACKER - RECORD YOUR END-MONTH NUMBERS, FANS, AND FOLLOWERS.

FB    PINTEREST    EMAIL    VIEWS    SALES    [        ]  [        ]  [        ]  [        ]

——————    ——————    ——————    ——————    ——————    ——————    ——————    ——————    ——————

*circle the metrics you will work to improve next month*

GOAL TRACKER - RECORD YOUR PROGRESS AND CHALLENGES THIS MONTH.

FINANCIAL:

SPIRITUAL:

MENTAL:

PHYSICAL:

RELATIONAL:

MOST IMPORTANT TO ME RIGHT NOW?

DOES MY SCHEDULE NEED REARRANGED?

PROFIT TRACKER - RECORD THIS MONTH'S INCOME, SALARY, AND EXPENSES.

TOTAL EARNED (YEAR-TO-DATE):

*December review*

## PROJECTS COMPLETED THIS MONTH

## WHAT WORKED WELL THIS MONTH?

### AND WHY?

HOW CAN I MULTIPLY THESE RESULTS?

## PROJECTS STILL IN THE WORKS

## DID THIS MONTH GET ME CLOSER TO MY ANNUAL OBJECTIVES?

IF YES, HOW WILL I KEEP UP THE MOMENTUM?

IF NO, WHAT WILL I DO TO GET BACK ON TRACK?

## WHAT OBSTACLE(S) AM I FACING?

WHY IS IT DIFFICULT?

HOW HAVE I TRIED TO OVERCOME IT?

WHAT CAN I TRY NEXT?

# YOUR ANNUAL STRATEGY

| JANUARY | FEBRUARY | MARCH | APRIL |
|---------|----------|-------|-------|

| MAY | JUNE | JULY | AUGUST |
|-----|------|------|--------|

| SEPTEMBER | OCTOBER | NOVEMBER | DECEMBER |
|-----------|---------|----------|----------|

*quarterly review*

WHAT ARE YOUR FAVORITE MEMORIES?

WHAT WAS TIME VERY WELL SPENT?

WHAT DID YOU ACCOMPLISH OR COMPLETE?

WHAT WAS MONEY VERY WELL SPENT?

HAVE YOU MADE PROGRESS ON YOUR ANNUAL OBJECTIVES?

WHAT ARE YOUR OUTSTANDING GOALS?

WHAT WAS YOUR WORST SETBACK?

ARE YOU KEEPING ANY BAD HABITS?

WHAT'S HOLDING YOU BACK?

# ✓ PRODUCTIVITY TIPS

You wear many hats in online business. Let's just stop and consider your day for a moment. If you're anything like me, you wake up and go over the day's schedule. You cover things like: what needs to be made, who needs to be replied to, what customers need to be served, and what meetings need to be attended. You're your own assistant.

Next, you launch into production. Your business requires assets to sell whether it's a handmade product or your next online training. You're the manufacturer.

Once that's done, it's time for you to engage! It's up to you to spread the word about your business and make sure your customers have new and exciting updates to look at. Facebook, Pinterest, Instagram, here you come! After all, you're the PR agent.

Now that you've gotten all that out of the way, it's time to get down to action. You have products to ship and requests to respond to. Your customers aren't going to serve themselves! You're the customer service representative.

Phew! It's been a long morning so far. After you've taken a lunch break and stretched your legs a bit, you've got to do a little planning for the coming month. There are books and a budget to keep. You have new projects to plan, supplies to order, and inventory to maintain because you're the office manager.

Hold on! Wait a second! You realize that those new designs aren't going to market themselves. You need an advertising strategy and a proactive plan to spread the word. Who's going to be interested in what you're creating? You have to draw up an ideal customer. Where's the person who wants this product hanging out? That's going to require some brainstorming. Add that to your to-do list because you're the VP of sales and marketing.

Time to wind down. The family's all home now, and that indicates a proper quitting time. You just need a few minutes of reflection to look over your to-do list. You ask yourself: *Am I doing a good job? Is this working? Am I wasting my precious resources or building something that will succeed? Have I done enough? Should I do more? Are the things I'm doing returning the results I want?* It's a solitary and quiet, sometimes somber moment. You have to look at your business — this thing you love and hold so close to your heart — from a bigger perspective because you're the CEO.

I point this out so you'll realize all that you do in a day! It's probably hard for your family and friends to understand, especially at first. To them, you always seem lost in a new product, your online storefront, or whatever else you're working on. Start-up ain't easy. Forgive me if I've ever given you a different impression; that's never my intention.

**"** ...WE ALWAYS ENVY OTHERS, COMPARING OUR SHADOWS TO THEIR SUNLIT SIDES.

*– Margaret George*

I find that anytime I feel overwhelmed in business, it's because I'm not wearing one of my many hats, overlooking some very important tasks.

## CREATE A ROUTINE THAT WORKS FOR YOU

Some people make magic with the "eat that frog" method — which means, they wake up and do the most daunting task on their list, and then finish whatever else needs doing. This works great for some, but I tend to let myself off easy once the biggest chore is finished. We all have to complete tasks that overwhelm or otherwise burden us. Try every method until you find the system that works best for you.

Here's how I schedule my day:

**5:30-6:40:** Wake up and perform administrative tasks over coffee. Some people vow to never check email in the morning, but I just want to! I record sales from the previous day into my abundance tracker, talk to Luminaries, check social, and look at stats if something big is going on.

**6:40-7:40:** Wake my children, prep their day, eat my breakfast, clean my kitchen, dress (for a workout), and ready my workspace.

**7:50-9:20:** Powerblock 1. This is determined by the weekly tasks that will make significant progress toward my goals. Right now, it's typically things such as, blog ahead, finish next project, or rehearse for CreativeLive. It is always something that will generate income for my business.

The #1 factor to a successful powerblock? No distractions. There are zero notifications set up on my phone and the ringer is on vibrate-only during work hours. Nobody has my home phone number except for my husband and children. I never give it out; I wouldn't take an uninvited phone call during my workday any sooner than a doctor would answer his phone during patient rounds.

**9:20-11:00:** Workout and shower. I used to put workouts at the end of the day, and more often than not, I had a reason *not to* workout at the end of the day. But this year, I was called to present myself, so I consider my hour-long workout everyday part of my job.

Plus, I just love how decadent I feel at 10:30 AM when I'm done with a workout and enjoying a hot shower on a Tuesday!

**11:00-12:00:** Admin and reset. After a good workout, I ease myself back into the workday, answering emails, having my lunch, and checking social.

**12:00-1:30:** Powerblock 2. If I finished a task in the first powerblock of the day, I'm onto the next thing on my weekly list. Again, and important to note, it is always something that will generate income for my business.

**1:30 - 2:30:** If I'm under a tight deadline or thoroughly engaged in my work, I reserve this window to finish up. If not, I'll use it for future business planning (because I'm the CEO) or administrative tasks (I'm also the secretary).

**2:30 - on:** The rest of my day is personal; I'll do an hour of house chores, reading, meditating, or snoozing before my children come home. I'm very much in-my-head during work hours, and I use this break to wind down and come back to Earth. However, if I'm very tuned into something or thoroughly engaged, I reserve this window for important deadlines.

I love the current routine I'm on, and I feel more productive than ever. I challenge you to create the same with whatever time you have to work on your business and improve your life.

I showed you mine, maybe you'd like to show me yours! I'd love to see a breakdown of your schedule and how you're using your planner. Remember to use the hashtag #YBY2017 on social so the community of *Your Best Year* planners can find your post.

## OUTSOURCE YOUR TASK LIST

The next tip is about hiring for your business, but don't get it twisted. This isn't about hiring for hiring's sake. If you're at all lost in logistics, or if you find yourself chasing different business advice all over the map, it's too early to hire. Save your money and the enormous chunk of time and energy it takes to feed your hire's position, and focus on your future strategy for success using the tools in this book.

Now that the disclaimer's out of the way, let's get right to the good stuff! At the start of online business, your working hours don't always generate income. The building, learning, and researching of it all must be done by you.

As your business grows, so will the income you earn with every hour invested. That start-up mentality can quickly become the bottleneck to your business' growth, as it did mine. This means that something you create is very valuable to your customer (thereby generating a substantial income), and you're trying to do it *and* everything else on your business to-do list, all by yourself.

Identify your #1 income-generator, then calculate how much you earn per hour you spend on that task. When the amount you earn on your #1 income-generator exceeds the cost of outsourcing other tasks, it's time to hire.

## WHAT'S YOUR #1 INCOME-GENERATOR?

For example, my number one income-generator is content (in the form of courses, books, and training). Consultation is a close second. When I'm doing either of these, I generate substantial hourly wages.

Next, organize all of your weekly tasks into one of three categories:

1. Work that creates income
2. Busywork to maintain your business
3. Your household responsibilities

This is the best exercise on the planet when you're thinking about hiring your first employee. To start, think of every task you do each week — your responsibilities in both your personal and professional life.

Then, decide which items you want to continue and which you'd like to eventually delegate. Here's a sample of my weekly tasks, organized into the three columns.

| KEY | | |
|---|---|---|
| • | MINE TO CONTINUE | |
| ○ | TASKS TO DELEGATE | |
| X | TASKS ALREADY DELEGATED | |

| *income-generating* WORK | *busy* WORK | *household* WORK |
|---|---|---|
| • blog | ○ branding | X ironing |
| • books | • video production | • laundry |
| • club | X video editing | X housecleaning |
| • courses | X webinar setup | • meal planning |
| • coaching | ○ accounting | • cooking |
| | ○ customer support | ○ grocery shopping |
| | X text proofread | |
| | X product shipping | |

As you can see, I organized everything that is my responsibility into the three aforementioned categories. In this example worksheet, I decided which tasks I want to continue (marked with a closed dot), which tasks I would like to give up (marked with an open dot), and which tasks I've already delegated (marked with an x).

*organize your task list*

| KEY |

MINE TO CONTINUE

TASKS TO DELEGATE

TASKS ALREADY DELEGATED

*income-generating*
WORK

*busy*
WORK

*household*
WORK

## IN CLOSING

The goals you've set for yourself with this workbook are what's required for your personal vision of success. The journey ahead of you is not the easiest choice, I assure you. I applaud your commitment and thank you for your courage and service! Your passion makes the whole world come more alive.

Should you ever feel like giving up, consider this story from *Think and Grow Rich*. Napolean Hill wrote of R.U. Darby, who invested in mining during the gold-rush days. He and his uncle had discovered an ore of gold and bought the equipment they needed to mine the land. As soon as they began drilling below the ore, they found that the vein of gold disappeared completely! They kept drilling to no avail, until they finally gave up hope and quit.

Mr. Darby sold the machinery to a junk man for a fraction of its cost. The junk man then called a mining engineer to evaluate the land, and the engineer calculated that the vein of gold would be found three feet from where Mr. Darby and his uncle had stopped drilling. When Mr. Darby quit, he was three feet away from striking millions of dollars worth of gold.

" MOST GREAT PEOPLE HAVE ATTAINED THEIR GREATEST SUCCESS JUST ONE STEP BEYOND THEIR GREATEST FAILURE.

*– Napoleon Hill*

This year, do things differently. Make bold choices and demolish the foundation of your comfort zone. Be interesting. Accomplish something that makes you unabashedly proud of yourself and then go brag about it. Come alive in your skin because you're made of energy. BE THAT LIFE. Create with it and let it flow through you without filter.

I'll be rooting for you every step of the way.

If you should need me, find me in my zone — talking shop and strategizing growth at www.marketyourcreativity.com. Be sure to share your results and cozy planning days with me using #yby2017. Here's to your best year yet.

Made in the USA
Middletown, DE
27 December 2016